Studies in English and American Literature, Linguistics, and Culture

STUDIES IN ENGLISH AND AMERICAN LITERATURE, LINGUISTICS, AND CULTURE

CAMDEN HOUSE
Columbia, South Carolina

Anaïs Nin and Her Critics

About *Literary Criticism in Perspective*

Books in the series *Literary Criticism in Perspective*, a sub-series in *Studies in English and American Literature, Linguistics, and Culture,* trace literary scholarship and criticism on major and neglected writers alike, or on a single major work, a group of writers, a literary school or movement. In so doing the authors — authorities on the topic in question who are also well-versed in the principles and history of literary criticism — address a readership consisting of scholars, students of literature at the graduate and undergraduate level, and the general reader. One of the primary purposes of the series is to illuminate the nature of literary criticism itself, to gauge the influence of social and historic currents on aesthetic judgments once thought objective and normative.

James Hardin, General Editor
Benjamin Franklin V, Editor for English and American Literature

Philip K. Jason

Anaïs Nin
and her Critics

CAMDEN HOUSE

Library of Congress Cataloging-in-Publication Data

Jason, Philip K., 1941-
   Anaïs Nin and her critics / Philip K. Jason.
      p.   cm.   -- (Studies in English and American literature, linguistics,
   and culture)
      Includes bibliographical references and index.
      ISBN 1-879751-41-0
      1. Nin, Anaïs, 1903-1977--Criticism and interpretation--History.
   I. Title.   II. Series.
   PS3527.I865Z73   1993
   818'.5209--dc20   92-43130
                                                                      CIP

75044

Contents

Preface

MY PURPOSE IN THE FOLLOWING CHAPTERS is to trace, describe, and assess the critical response to Anaïs Nin's work. While a single, subdivided chronology might have served this purpose, I have opted for a series of separate, overlapping chronologies that attend to critical responses grouped by subject. That is, rather than choosing a span of years to delimit a chapter, I have chosen a significant shared purpose or topic of the criticism. This plan, I believe, provides a more readable narrative and helps sharpen the presentation of critical debate.

For the most part, the selection of commentary on Nin's work addressed here is that which has appeared in books and academic or cultural journals. Book reviews have been considered only selectively and characterized briefly, and then usually for the earlier decades of Nin's career when they have been the only available form of commentary. Rose Marie Cutting's *Anaïs Nin: A Reference Guide* (1978) has been a most useful tool in locating reviews and must be consulted by students who require further references of this kind. Ill-equipped as a translator, I have limited the scope of this survey (with some few exceptions) to criticism in English. However, there is a sizeable and growing body of criticism on Nin's work in several other languages. Overviews of Nin's reputation in other language communities are mentioned in chapter 2. Theses and dissertations are excluded from this study on the assumption that the most persuasive and significant of these efforts have found their way into journals and books and are recognized in that form.

Like other titles in the *Literary Criticism in Perspective* series, this study is attentive to the ways in which literary criticism reflects social and historical forces, whether consciously or through unarticulated assumptions. This study also aims to point out how (and how much) the body of criticism has accomplished in orienting readers to the canonical possibilities of Nin's writing by elucidating their themes, structures, and techniques. In Nin's case, the critical tapestry reveals a fascinating weave of writings that address her literary achievement and writings that address her status as an exemplary figure. Her works and days are often presented as evidenciary materials for feminist polemic and psychoanalytical casework. Influence and affinity studies abound, while detailed stylistic analyses are rare. If schools and kinds of literary criticism are distinguished by the kinds of questions they valorize, one must assume, in Nin's case and in others, that critical endeavor seeks as its subject those authors and writings most responsive to its favored questions.

Thanks are due to the Naval Academy Research Council for financial assistance; to the reference staff of the Nimitz Library, USNA, for a wide range of support services; and to my friend and colleague Jonathan Eller for helping with the preparation of photo-ready copy. Most of all, and as always, I thank my wife Ruth for her countless acts of loving-kindness and for her patient bearing of those inevitably lonely passages in the life of a reclusive scholar's spouse.

For convenience, titles of Nin's works are often abbreviated as follows:

Anaïs Nin Reader	*Reader*
Children of the Albatross	*Children*
Cities of the Interior	*Cities*
D. H. Lawrence: An Unprofessional Study	*Lawrence*
Delta of Venus	*Delta*
The Diary of Anaïs Nin	*Diary*
The Early Diary of Anaïs Nin	*Early Diary*
The Four-Chambered Heart	*Heart*
Henry and June	*H&J*
House of Incest	*House*
Ladders to Fire	*Ladders*
The Novel of the Future	*Novel*
Seduction of the Minotaur	*Seduction*
A Spy in the House of Love	*Spy*
Under a Glass Bell	*Bell*
Winter of Artifice	*Winter*
"Winter of Artifice"	"Winter"

1: Issues in Nin Criticism

Two of the major issues in Nin criticism may be addressed separately, but are finally related. The first of these has to do with the relative status and value of the *Diary* versus the fiction. All students of Nin's work recognize the dependence of the fiction on the diary, a dependence that is attested to in Nin's own comments. Some, Nancy Scholar for example, see the *Diary* volumes as Nin's main accomplishment, the fiction a pale, sporadically effective, largely undistinguished echo. Others see the fiction as Nin's primary literary achievement. These latter critics seem to share an assumption about the relative status of the endeavors that valorizes fiction at the expense of nonfiction. That is, the question is not so much whether Nin is a more effective writer in one form than another as it is the inherent (or should I say traditional) status of the genres as literary kinds. The elevated status of literary nonfiction in recent decades – a status ushered in by such phenomena as the new journalism, the nonfiction novel, and the interest that feminist criticism has taken in autobiographical modes – helps make the higher valuing of Nin's *Diary* possible for some of her readers.

The second issue, which primarily concerns her achievement as a fiction writer, derives, in part, from Nin's own thematic obsessions and the nature of the vehicles she has created to convey them. On the thematic level of exploration of the self, the issue may be stated as unity versus multiplicity (and its complicating correlative: stasis versus flow). The issue for criticism becomes whether to stress the individual integrity of Nin's several titles and assess them individually, even while noting their relationships, or to explore her work comprehensively as a single organic achievement, even while noting its subdivisions or phases. *Cities of the Interior*, billed and perhaps even conceived as a "continuous novel," is Nin's major attempt to establish the latter perspective.

The issues become related as soon as one recognizes that it is almost impossible to treat Nin's *Diary* as anything else but a continuous, single work whose division into volumes is primarily a publishing convenience. (However, this perspective would discount the shaping editorial hand or hands that, to some, have remade diary into autobiography.) The *Diary of Anaïs Nin*, along with its excrescences by way of alternative "fictional" formulations, may also be reasonably explored as an *oeuvre* (much like a self with many stages and/or masks). The traditions of literary criticism, it must be said, favor the work-by-work approach; indeed, they favor chronology in career studies.

As we shall see, the organizational and other strategies of the six book-length studies on Nin reflect these two fundamental issues. Four of them – the ones by Oliver Evans (1968), Bettina L. Knapp (1978), Benjamin Franklin V and Duane Schneider (1979), and Scholar (1984) – treat the fiction title by title. The other two – by Evelyn J. Hinz (1971, rev. 1973) and Sharon Spencer (1977, rev. 1981) – organize by critical issues of method and theme, cutting across the works to illustrate various points, consequently never exploring any individual title in full. Each of the six critics finds it necessary to treat the *Diary* separately from the fiction, but placement and emphasis vary from study to study.[1]

Another issue in Nin criticism stems from the popularity of the Anaïs Nin presented in the *Diary* (and in public forums in her later years) as well as from Nin's theme, registered there and elsewhere, of self-creation. For many readers and partisans, Nin is not so much to be praised for the literary value of her writings as she is to be admired as an exemplary figure – a model of feminine self-making in a world in which women's roles are histor- ically defined by men. Not only is her life struggle a model on the most gen- eral plane, but also on the very specific one of artist or writer. For many, Nin's importance is in her *career*, not in her achievement; that is, to be Ar- noldian for a moment, Nin and her writings have a special historical impor- tance, though perhaps only modest value in absolute terms.

Of course, raising the spirit of Arnold reminds us of the issue we are nearing: the recognition of a male-defined set of standards for judging liter- ary value, a male-centered tradition, and a notion of "absolute" that means "masculine." For those who argue the existence of a distinctive feminine sensibility and the possibility of a uniquely feminine writing (with its own agendas and standards), Nin frequently ranks as a landmark or "break- through" writer. At worst, she is a valiant experimenter and an enabler for others. It is no wonder, then, that her *Diary* – defined by feminist criticism as a female mode – brings her accolades that are not accorded to her fiction. Note, however, that some prominent feminist critics are quite hostile to- ward Nin and her writings.

The most frequently addressed issue in Nin criticism is the *ism* issue. If we were only sure which *ism* to attach her work to, then we would be able to give Nin her due. Nin, and many of her partisans, position her as a writer defiant of the tenets and assumptions of realism (which some argue carry an excess of masculine baggage). Because Nin's work fails the tests of verisi- militudinous realism, some assume it is nonsense, some assume it is signifi- cant work being misread or inappropriately approached, and some think that Nin's combinations of surrealist, symbolist, lyrical, and psychological techniques are either intriguing or obscure in theory but in any case second- rate work.

Interestingly, two of the critics who are Nin's best explainers with regard to an esthetic orientation, Evelyn J. Hinz and Sharon Spencer, are also the authors of the two studies that are structured to embrace the whole of Nin's achievement rather than to address individual works. Fittingly, theirs are the only studies metaphorically titled. Because of the special orientation of these two books, and because they help to put in focus several of the key critical issues, they receive detailed treatment in this chapter; the other four studies receive significant attention in later chapters where the commentaries on individual works are reviewed.

Hinz's *The Mirror and Garden: Realism and Reality in the Writings of Anaïs Nin*, first published in 1971 and then in a revised version (which adds comment on volume 4 of the *Diary*) in 1973, came at a time when Nin's popular reputation was at its height – though much more for the *Diary* than for the fiction. Nevertheless, the orientation of Hinz's study is to open doors for more readers – and possibly for more academics – and to emphasize the fiction by treating it in its own literary dimension and not in terms of its relationship to the *Diary* material. One strategy Hinz employs is strikingly conservative; rather than making Nin out to be the latest version of the latest fashion or a forerunner of literary fashions yet to come (as Oliver Evans does in his earlier study), Hinz creates a web of allusions and analogies that places Nin inside accessible, sanctioned traditions. We do not find much about scary foreigners like Artaud and Breton. There is more reference to Henry James than to André Gide, more to Emerson than to Rimbaud and Lautréamont combined, and more to the distant and hallowed past than to the unsettled present.

At the same time, Hinz tries to defend and dignify Nin's best understanding of her own ends. The title metaphor of Hinz's work is patiently developed both theoretically and in application to Nin's fictional enterprise. The mirror, we learn, is the symbol of and for the deterministic social realists who value and reflect only the surface. Set against this icon for "realism" is the garden, representing the organic nature of "reality" in which change and adaptation take place. The second symbol is not promising, carrying as it does associations of artifice – of "nature methodized" – which are far from Nin's or Hinz's point of emphasis; but Hinz's discussion makes the best of it.

Hinz's book, then, advances Nin's notion of reality in life and in art, and Hinz argues that an understanding of this perspective is the most useful key to Nin's fiction. Thus, Hinz gives Nin's own efforts in criticism detailed attention here, much more than any other critic gives them. Hinz's careful analysis of Nin's first book, *D. H. Lawrence: An Unprofessional Study*, reveals it to be a "subjective criticism" in which Nin tells us less about how to read Lawrence and more about how to read what she herself will eventually write. Hinz also attends to *The Novel of the Future* and to Nin's short "credo" essays of the 1940s. She does not make the mistake of claiming great critical acumen for Nin. Rather, Hinz uses these works primarily to help us grasp Nin's intentions as an artist, and she succeeds extremely well (though the argument always exists that Nin's intentions are irrelevant to measuring her achievement).

The body of Hinz's discussion investigates four aspects of Nin's art and connects each to the underlying "garden/reality" credo. These are themes, structure, characters, and language.

For Hinz, Nin's broadest theme may be stated as "woman at war with herself," a struggle that can have positive or destructive consequences. Underlying either pattern is another concept, "karma," which views outcomes as exactly appropriate to deeds. The karmic principle also demands that patterns of sin and retribution be repeated until the individual comes to understand their meaning. Finally, karmic justice promotes the search for self-knowledge and the transcendence of false selves. Related to karma as controlling ideas in Nin's fiction are tropism and fixation. "Tropism" is defined as creative change, Nin's sense of the healthy individual's ability to adapt and grow. Destruction, on the other hand, "is the symptom and effect of fixation" (40). Hinz traces the operation of karmic justice in emblems and episodes from a wide range of Nin's fiction, employing a nonclinical language to elucidate what is essentially Nin's psychoanalytic theme.

In contrast to the chronological narrative pattern of the conventional novel with its "linear and historical concept of time" (50), Nin offers a continuous flow in which the conscious and unconscious interact. The locale of Nin's fiction "is not the phenomenal but the noumenal world" (53) in which emotion and memory, not the clock or the outer seasons, dictate the sequence of occurrences. Images and symbols are structural devices in Nin's work; thus, her novels (individually and collectively) often have the quality of dream and have more in common with lyric poetry than with traditional prose fiction. Hinz alerts readers, finally, to the "canonical form" of Nin's stories and novels taken together: the individual titles are variations or phases of the central canonical themes which are given different emphasis not so much from work to work but by their different manifestations within Nin's reappearing characters. The long journey taken in the *roman fleuve* is characterized by a movement from inner to outer, subjectivity to objectivity, both in terms of the narrator's vision and Nin's technique.

In examining Nin's characters – rather, her methods of characterization – Hinz is at her most imaginative. To establish a defining contrast with the "laboratorical" method of characterization in realistic and especially naturalistic fiction, Hinz holds up the precedent of the *Psychomachia* of Prudentius and the Christian morality plays of the Middle Ages. These analogies allow Hinz to lend dignity to Nin's flat, abstract characters. "In the modern *psychomachia* of Nin," Hinz argues, "personifications of the basic passions battle for supremacy in the female psyche" (63). Hinz goes on to observe, quite convincingly, that through her four main female characters Nin externalizes and dramatizes the internal conflicts of womankind. Each aspect of woman becomes a type, vibrating with mythic overtones. Each enacts a phase of the struggle of woman at war with herself; collectively, they dramatize the struggle on a grand scale. In Nin, moral and psychological typing are linked as well as underscored by symbolic details of appearance. Hinz argues that by usually choosing not to give her characters surnames (Lillian Beye is the exception), Nin further insists on their representative natures.

Hinz explores Nin's use of language in a chapter called "Bread and the Wafer," borrowing a subsection title from Nin's *Ladders to Fire*. Nin objects to both the language of mere denotative accuracy and the language of intellectual abstraction. In her art, Hinz explains, Nin's goal is emotional accuracy. To this end, she uses techniques that approach stream of consciousness but which pay special attention to prose rhythms. Rhythm becomes a device of characterization and of sensual life: "Since the most basic rhythms of life are those of pulse and copulation, Nin experiments with ways of making the sexual encounters of her heroines rhythmically perceptible" (78). Sensuous diction, image-laden phrasing, and provocative sound patterns combine with rhythmical shaping in Nin's evocations of emotional and physical states. Although like any writer Nin is sometimes capable of an exaggeration of style that misfires into self-parody, most often she controls her devices well. Her preference for the unconventional word choice or unexpected allusion involves risks that do not always pay off and sometimes lead to literal inaccuracies, but we must remember that Nin's search for precision is always first in the service of emotional accuracy. With such formulations, Hinz addresses Nin's goals and practices as a prose stylist, recognizing the limitations of Nin's art while continuing to develop a context that makes most of what Nin does acceptable, even admirable.

Hinz's final chapter is on the *Diary* volumes. Here, however, her method undergoes an ironic shift. Instead of a discussion that subordinates the individual volumes to a more comprehensive notion of Nin's achievement in this area, Hinz, after some introductory comments in which she examines the respective roles of diary and fiction in treating identical themes, discusses the first four volumes one at a time. In fact, she performs the kind of content summary ("plot" is not an appropriate term here) and structural appraisal that one expects to be an element in the assessment of individual works of fiction – the very approach she steers clear of in the main and most useful part of her book.

After (in her revised edition) treating the fourth volume, Hinz chooses to let her study dissolve into ellipses. There is no conclusion, no recapitulation or final bringing together of main issues. Indeed, it is Hinz's penultimate chapter on *The Novel of the Future* that carries with it the sense of an ending. Obviously, Hinz felt an obligation to discuss the *Diary* in her study of *all* of Nin's work then available, but the placement and character of the *Diary* discussion makes it seem just that – an obligation, not a task Hinz was inspired to perform. Though the justification of reflecting Nin's own spirit of openendedness is available (and one must remember that Hinz was properly anticipating additions to the Nin canon), the fadeout is an unsatisfactory close to a book that in many ways is more than satisfactory.

Hinz succeeds admirably in providing readers with a brief, lucid, yet comprehensive approach to Nin's writing. And she was the first to do so (Evans only treats the fiction). No one has explored Nin's critical formulations with greater insight or sensitivity. Hinz offers serviceable ways of reading Nin, though without ever quite providing a full-blown application of these critical tools. Her manner is dignified, her enthusiasm partially masked by a formal, academic stance somewhat at war with the values she praises in her subject. Moreover, Hinz's wide-ranging and often eclectic allusions leave Nin spread out over time and space; at once European-medieval, Asian-karmic (as domesticated by transcendental thought and hippie style), and Emersonian, Nin has little chance of emerging as the product of a distinctive cultural climate.[2]

Sharon Spencer's *Collage of Dreams: The Writing of Anaïs Nin* (1977) shares many of the broad assumptions of Hinz's book. Spencer, too, believes that Nin's work is best confronted as a whole rather than in its individual parts. She also focuses individual chapters on themes and techniques, working toward demonstrating a synthesis between the two. Though the *Diary* looms larger in Spencer's study than in Hinz's (in part because there are by this time six volumes in print), it still follows the fiction in order of discussion. However, Spencer minimizes the issue of distance between the genres by pointing out that none of Nin's work fits neatly into genre categories. Thus, Spencer is able to consider Nin's "writing" in an even more holistic way than Hinz does. More than Hinz, Spencer sets Nin in her own time, building connections between Nin's art and the larger world of modernist expression. Finally, Spencer stresses the interaction between Nin's life and her work, accepting the notion that there is no clear line between the job of evaluating the one and that of evaluating the other.

For Spencer, the theme of Nin's life and work is "transformation." Her opening chapter, "The Art of Rag-Picking," centers on this theme as it is developed in Nin's early story "Ragtime," which suggests that the various bits and pieces of detritus that the ragpicker salvages are refashioned, recycled, and made into something new just as an artist's memories, dreams, and materials (including language) are transformed into the artwork. It is a short imaginative step for Spencer to connect this motif with the title and technique of Nin's last fictional narrative, *Collages*, which pieces together various narrative patches in a self-conscious adaptation of technique from the visual arts. Spencer points out the popularity of collage expression among the surrealists whom Nin admired in her formative years as an artist. Rag-picking and collage serve not only as an approach to any particular Nin title, they provide a way of looking at the totally of Nin's literary output – a single collage work.

In her next chapter, "Symphonic Writing," Spencer further explores the relationships between Nin's literary techniques and those of other arts. Since Nin was born into a family of musicians, one might expect the profound influence of music on Nin's writing. Spencer examines how Nin's affinity with the symbolists is not only apparent in her symbolic style and in her use of dream and fantasy, but also in her use of music as inspiration. For such writers, the goal of literature is to approximate music. "All her life," writes Spencer, "Nin has sought to musicalize her writing" (20). Musical images, metaphors, and allusions – and lush orchestrations of language – characterize much of Nin's work, and Spencer points them out in admirable detail. She also underscores the ways in which Nin's compositions borrow musical structures.

The aspiration toward music is an aspiration toward fluidity and continuity and away from materiality and fixity. Just as music cannot describe, "Nin does not describe. She interprets, and in the act of interpretation she re-creates her subjects over and over again . . ." (23). Just as music "evokes and transmits memory by the process of association of sensory images," so Nin works to provide a cluster of associations in her writing (41).

Spencer is also interested in how Nin responds to certain kinds of painting, sculpture, and dance. She explores Nin's attempts to transform elements of these several arts into literature, though dance receives the most attention. Spencer illustrates how Nin uses dance metaphorically and (in the form of gesture) as a device of characterization. Moreover, Nin attempts to find structures akin to the choreography of Martha Graham and other creators of modern dance. Openness (or open-endedness) and the gathering together of seemingly unrelated parts are everywhere the hallmarks of Nin's art as a writer. Spencer shows most clearly how Nin's search for models leads her not only to literary figures like Proust, but also to a wide range of nonliterary inspirations. In so doing, Spencer means to help the reader locate Nin's strengths, but it is fair to say that these same tendencies are the source of Nin's weaknesses as well.

Nin's complex relationship to the concept and ideal of the dream is the subject of Spencer's next chapter. The connecting tissue of fluidity and transformation links this concern with those previously addressed. Spencer stresses Nin's pragmatic orientation toward dreams, which must be used and built upon, both in life and in art. For Nin, as Spencer explains, psychoanalysis is the key, the discipline and philosophy of life, that allows her to tap her unconscious in a creative and practical way. The details of characterization that some find lacking in Nin's work, Spencer argues, are only the details of the half-life of consciousness. Nin explores both the conscious and subconscious dimensions of her characters, giving the latter a prominence found in few other writers.

Spencer notes the important influence on Nin of her own therapists as well as her independent adaptation of the teachings and methods of each.

What Nin came to believe about the processes of personal growth become, in a sense, the "plots" of her fictions, and Spencer offers brief examinations of these processes as delineated through some of Nin's major characters. She observes this basic pattern: "In Nin's work, as in Hesse's, a disintegration of personality typically precedes a new alignment of elements into a new being" (66). Much of this process takes place below the level of consciousness; much of the work of remaking is done in dreams. Without delving into the reality of dreams, then, Nin could never present the process of transformation as she understood it.

Understanding is both a cause and effect of transformation, and for Nin understanding herself as a woman has the highest priority. One of Spencer's many contributions to Nin studies is to articulate clearly and at some length the proto-feminist impulse in Nin's life and work. The chapter "Rediscovering Woman" is the center of this discussion. Here, Spencer reviews Nin's experience and expression of the stultifying role of mother, opening the discussion beyond Nin and her work, but always returning to a fruitful analysis of how Nin addresses such key issues of gender in her writings. Trained to give, to nurture, and to repress her own (sexual) nature by the patriarchal dynamic of Judeo-Christian culture generally and her traditional Roman Catholic upbringing in particular, Nin fought her private struggle for liberation and voiced it for herself and other women in her writings.

Spencer traces the workings of divided female selves in the stories of Lillian, Sabina, and Djuna that wind through the *Cities of the Interior* novels and in some of Nin's shorter fictions. Each woman struggles with some version of the father-daughter relationship in a way that affects her adult relationships with male partners and potential partners. Each seeks a "fuller, more developed, and more powerful" (83) self freed from the guilt of not fulfilling those internalized, learned behaviors of mothering. Each seeks a unity that is not stasis and a coequal status with men that is rooted in an honest, open, femininity. Each needs to overcome the need for depending on a father's (or father figure's) approval in her quest for a feeling of self-worth.

Spencer succeeds remarkably in developing these issues and illustrating Nin's inventive probing of the dilemmas of modern womanhood. She explores the Jungian underpinning of Nin's "expansive" view of woman, comments exuberantly on Nin's daring in the portrayal of sensual and sexual feeling and behavior, and drives home the theme of Nin's characters' "striving to attain the ideal state of emotional and sexual synthesis" or balance in a world that still restricts woman's "opportunities for fulfillment without censure" (92).

From these general concerns, Spencer turns in her next chapter to the somewhat more limited but equally prominent one of "the psychological obstacles woman must overcome when she defines herself as an artist" (94). This section, called "Transforming the Muse," sensitively traces Nin's relationship with various mentors and models and her own gradual emergence as one who chose to forsake (at some cost) a range of conventional nurturing relationships in order to direct her energies to creativity. In Jungian terms, "The recognition of her animus demanded that she put increasing emphasis on her commitment to writing at the risk of sacrificing personal relationships" (109). Spencer also examines the conflict between creative and procreative roles and probes the meaning of Nin's friendships with homosexual writers and artists, connecting it to Nin's need to bring "both masculine and feminine components of the self into the sort of awareness that can result in changed actions" (109). She offers, as well, an articulation of Nin's goals as a self-styled "feminine" writer: "Feminine art restores connections with nature; instead of dominating her materials, the artist coaxes them to reveal their essences" (111).

In these last two chapters, then, Spencer attends more to portraying Nin's life-themes, her personal struggles, and less to interpreting and assessing Nin's writing. She employs the writings themselves as evidence of Nin's concerns. Here and elsewhere, *Collage of Dreams* becomes more a portrait of Nin as exemplary figure than an exercise in traditional literary criticism. Spencer pursues Nin as the Ur-character in Nin's major creative project: her own self.

From here it is a natural step to "Anaïs: Her Book," the first of two chapters on the *Diary*. To her credit (and consistent with her method elsewhere), Spencer views this work less as a series of volumes than as a total work and process. Nonetheless, she enunciates the separate themes of the several *Diary* volumes. Speculations about genre and intriguing details regarding Nin's evolving attitude toward the *Diary* fill this chapter. In the next, "The 'Journal des Autres,' " Spencer discusses the broad themes and methods of the *Diary*, the acclaim it has received, and the various reasons for that acclaim. Her observations will be treated in detail along with other critical studies of Nin's greatest success.

In closing, Spencer takes up the issue of narcissism. To defend Nin from the frequent charge of an excessive, even morbid, self-concern, Spencer traces the history of literary uses of the Narcissus myth to suggest other values. She reviews, as well, the Rankian thesis of self-affirmation that is an important step in the making of any artist. Spencer argues that the *Diary* records Nin's working through the necessary phase of narcissism as a prelude to creative work and a foundation for offering love to others. An examination of Nin's use of water imagery concludes this discussion of how Nin's art is embracing and encompassing rather than insular and exclusive.

One of the superior features of Spencer's book is the very structural method she has developed. The chapters of the book form a collage of essays, each of which can be read as a self-contained exposition of one or another aspect of Nin's work (and many of which grow out of separately published articles). Yet each gains from its relationship to the others, deepening, heightening, accenting, echoing, building toward a carefully orchestrated whole. In this way, Spencer creates a facsimile in criticism of the very techniques and issues she addresses, and she does it quite well.

The drawback of the book is its unrelieved boosterism. Spencer is too close to Nin, too much in thrall of her subject. Though an able scholar, Spencer too often leans toward what Hinz calls the subjective criticism of Nin's own critical prose, producing an effort that is always in the service of protecting and honoring. It shares with the other early studies an excess of enthusiasm, and perhaps outdoes them in this regard. Nevertheless, as a self-confessed "daughter of Anaïs," Spencer has, in pursuit of the mother, mastered the teachings and writings of those who influenced Nin in a thorough and productive way.[3]

The highly partisan, enthusiast tradition has been a mixed blessing for Nin's status in academic circles. On the one hand, without the ardent efforts of a handful of dedicated Nin devotees, the means of access to Nin's art and significance may have never come or been postponed even longer. On the other hand, the narrow circle of enthusiasts has often seemed to be writing under a jealously maintained glass bell. Resisting or failing to move out boldly into the broader streams of academic discourse, Nin criticism has been cloistered in special houses where family manners required applause and assent and where a kind of incestuous siblinghood reigned, with Nin herself (almost until her death) a guiding and contributing intelligence. This situation, though modified, still exists and the present work does not claim to escape it.

We must observe, for example, that a disproportionate number of the biographical and critical essays about Nin are to be found in four periodicals and three anthologies. Three of these periodicals were specifically designed to foster and maintain interest in Nin's life and work. *Under the Sign of Pisces: Anaïs Nin and Her Circle* appeared quarterly from 1970 through 1981. Endorsed by Nin, this publication, primarily a newsletter, was edited by Richard Centing and Benjamin Franklin V, with Centing taking over the sole burden in its later years. Centing continued his mission with *Seahorse: The Anaïs Nin/Henry Miller Journal* which ran quarterly for two years beginning in 1982. Both periodicals are mines of context for Nin studies, mixing news, short critical pieces, and bibliographical material. Beginning in 1983, *Anaïs: An International Journal* has been published by the Anaïs Nin Trust and edited by Gunther Stuhlmann. Attractively produced and hospitable to somewhat longer critical pieces, this annual continues as the institutionalized home of Nin studies. Stuhlmann, Nin's long-time editor-agent, keeps the doors more widely open than one might imagine as he presides over accretions of new prose about Nin and makes out-of-print and never-before-in-print memorabilia available.

The fourth journal to which Nin studies is indebted is the *Journal of the Otto Rank Association*. Properly seeing literary embodiments of Rank's ideas in Nin's writings, this periodical has frequently provided space to the examination of that fruitful interaction. Begun in 1966, the early volumes of *JORA* contain some of Nin's writings about Rank. Through the 1970s, writings about Nin herself or the Rank/Nin connection appear frequently, with Sharon Spencer's being the most important voice.

The theme of special homes and special occasions is maintained when we look at the three harvests of Nin criticism – or, rather, when we observe how little else about Nin has found its way into print. The special issue of *Mosaic* edited by Evelyn J. Hinz and titled *The World of Anaïs Nin* (1978) is the richest of the three. It is surrounded by Robert Zaller's *A Casebook on Anaïs Nin* (1974) and Sharon Spencer's *Anaïs, Art and Artists* (1986), both of which – while providing some important comment – are tilted more toward adulation than toward critical objectivity.

Writings about Nin make only rare appearances in established journals of literary and cultural criticism. In historical or thematic critical anthologies and monographs, comment about her work is similarly infrequent. However, over the last dozen or so years, the frequency of such appearances has accelerated. One can speculate about what would have happened if the energies put into building and appointing the paper shrines for Nin study had been put to a different, outward-reaching strategy.

A closer look at the main body of critical work reveals that in certain cases Nin's publishers have become her critics' publishers. Such a linkage is understandable and, in isolated occurrences, not unusual, but the patterns here raise questions about conflict of interest. Swallow Press, the standard publisher of Nin's fiction, also published Sharon Spencer's study (and a paperback reprint of her earlier book, *Space, Time and Structure in the Modern Novel*, which places Nin's work in the context of spatial form). The revised version of *Collage of Dreams*, expanded to include a chapter on Nin's erotica, was published by Harcourt Brace Jovanovich – publisher of the erotica. Soon after Swallow had become an imprint of Ohio University Press, the parent publisher released the study by Franklin and Schneider. The first edition of Hinz's book was published by the same Ohio State University Libraries Publications Committee through which Richard Centing published the Nin-endorsed newsletter. The expanded edition was published by Harcourt Brace Jovanovich, Nin's publisher for the *Diary*.

These facts, and others, may suggest that Nin herself had some influence on the critical enterprise, if only by force of personality. At best, one can say that Nin's own publishers were on key occasions the path of least resistance for critical discussions of her work. The trend in the criticism, at least in the book-length studies, is from works of enthusiasm and adulation (though Evans's is a bit more temperate than the three that follow) to works of cautious and limited praise. The volume by Franklin and Schneider (1979) and the later one by Scholar (1984) are the only two completed at some distance from Nin's death.[4] Whether they could have been published in Nin's life-time is an open question.

Notes to Chapter 1

[1]For successive studies, more *Diary* volumes were available. The ongoing publication of the *Diary* during the major years of the critical enterprise is a factor with important consequences for the assumptions and methods of the various studies.

[2] My first thoughts on Hinz's book are found in "The Future of Nin Criticism, A Review" (1972). Hinz reflects on her book and her critical stance in "The Creative Critic," found in Valerie Harms's *Celebration with Anaïs Nin* (1973).

[3]My earlier comments on Spencer's study appear in *Style* (1978).

[4]Published in the year following Nin's death, Knapp's book is solidly enthusiastic. No doubt Nin knew of and approved its general nature. Nin could be extremely loyal to her partisans, hostile toward those who could not find only splendor, as comments in *The Diary of Anaïs Nin, 1966-1974* amply illustrate. "Agreed to write a preface for *Harvard Advocate's* number on 'Women's Writing' only if they included Marguerite Young, Marianne Hauser, Anna Balakian, Sharon Spencer, and Bettina Knapp" (207). Reactions to work by Franklin and Scholar (Nancy Zee at the time) show Nin in a snit. Scholar's "cold-blooded thesis," the basis for her later book, upset her mightily, as did contributions to *Under the Sign of Pisces* by its coeditor, Franklin, "a totally negative critic" who "disparaged my friends" (289). Evans's little bit of fault-finding was also dismaying: "I was crushed by his lack of understanding. We exchanged bitter letters. I had let him interview me and had given him all the keys" (35). Of course, Evans was independent enough to refuse some of these keys and hold onto his own "Victorian and academic" perspective. Affectionate comments about Evelyn Hinz abound. Scholar takes her swing at the "exclusively advocatory stance" of Hinz, Spencer, and Knapp in her "Anaïs Nin Under a Glass Bell" (1981), a generally favorable review of Franklin and Schneider's volume.

2: Bibliography, Biography, and General Assessments

Bibliography

CONSIDERING THAT NIN IS ON no consensus list of major authors, it is surprising to find the extent to which attention has been paid to bibliographical matters. Particularly in the 1970s and early 1980s, bibliographers were busy providing other scholars with the foundation information regarding what Nin published when and what was published about her.

Most prominent among the achievements in bibliography is Benjamin Franklin V's *Anaïs Nin: A Bibliography* (1973). Published as number 29 in the prestigious Serif Series from Kent State University Press, Franklin's volume is a descriptive bibliography of Nin's published writings divided into five sections, each arranged chronologically: books and pamphlets, contributions to books, contributions to periodicals, Nin's recordings, and her editorship of periodicals. Because Nin's publishing history is complicated – a mixture of privately printed limited editions, large commercial house imprints, various editions and states of the same title, titles with changing contents, and texts with changing titles – Franklin's bibliography provides much more than publication history. Indeed, it provides vivid insights into the shifting fortunes and creative reconsiderations of Nin as she builds her literary career.[1]

A bibliography for a living writer is quite obviously out of date as soon as it goes to press. Many Nin titles appeared during the remainder of her life and thereafter. Thus, Franklin's effort is now seriously dated, though upon publication it met the highest standards of thoroughness and accuracy. In order to keep readers informed about Nin's "post-Franklin" publications, Richard R. Centing compiled a series of updates. These appear in *Under the Sign of Pisces: Anaïs Nin and Her Circle* beginning with the Spring 1974 issue (as "New Nin Publications") and continue until that periodical gives way to Centing's next project, *Seahorse: The Anaïs Nin / Henry Miller Journal*. Volume 1, number 3 (1982) of *Seahorse* continues the effort as "Primary Nin," which appears for its second and final time in volume 2, number 4 (1983). The most important of the Franklin updates is Reesa Marcinczyk's "A Checklist of the Writings of Anaïs Nin, 1973-1976," which appears in *Pisces* 8.1 (1977). Centing's less consequential "Blurbs by Anaïs Nin" is found in four parts: *Pisces* (Spring 1973), *Pisces* (Summer/Fall 1981), *Seahorse* 1.3 (1982), and *Seahorse* 1.4 (1982).

For the history of Nin's works in non-English editions, one must consult Gunther Stuhlmann's "Into Another Language: Some Notes on Anaïs Nin's Work in Translation" (1983). Stuhlmann traces Nin's reputation abroad, commenting on the early Dutch, Swedish, and Italian editions of her writings, other Scandinavian language editions, Eastern European and Japanese editions, and finally the Spanish and French editions which had particular significance for Nin given her heritage. In closing, he notes the growing interest in Nin's work throughout the German language community.

The applications of Franklin's detailed bibliographical research were made first and foremost by Franklin himself. His "Anaïs Nin: A Bibliographical Essay" (1974) organizes the essential bibliographical problems in Nin scholarship under three headings and provides a concise, lucid discussion of each. These are "Titles with Changing Contents," "Compositions with Changing Titles," and "Titles Referring to More Than One Work." Without taking advantage of Franklin's findings, Nin scholars are almost certainly doomed to error.

One of Franklin's warnings has to do with textual variants. His own "The Textual Evolution of the First Section of 'Houseboat' " (1978) is a model discussion of Nin's habits of revision.

An earlier textual study, Robert A. Tibbetts's "The Text of *On Writing*" (1973), compares two typescripts and the two published editions of Nin's essay. The same author's "*A Spy in the House of Love*: A Note on the First Printings" (1977) discovers twenty-two variants between the first (Dutch) and second (American) printings of that novel. The discrepancies here are the result of misprints in the first printing.

Nancy Scholar's "A Checklist of Nin Materials at Northwestern University Library" (1972) lists in outline form the materials then available. Marie-Claire Van der Elst's "The Manuscripts of Anaïs Nin at Northwestern University" (1978) characterizes in greater detail the ten boxes of manuscript material, comprising almost all of Nin's fiction (both published and unpublished) in that collection. She also notes two drafts toward *D. H. Lawrence: An Unprofessional Study*. Van der Elst comments on the glimpses of the creative process available from the examination of these manuscripts, and she gives some examples.

Bibliography turns into biography in various narratives of Nin's publishing history. Duane Schneider tells one such story in "The Duane Schneider Press and Anaïs Nin" (1973). Nin's Paris publications are effectively treated in those sections of Hugh Ford's *Published in Paris* (1975) that deal with Edward Titus's Black Manikin press and Jack Kahane's Guardian Obelisk. Gunther Stuhlmann pays proper tribute to Ford and to Titus in "Edward Titus Et Al." (1989), occasioned by the paperback reissue of Ford's book.

Two essays concentrate on Nin's activities as a publisher. Sally Dennison's "Anaïs Nin: The Book as a Work of Art" (1984) concerns itself with Nin's decision to publish her own writings and explores the function of the

Gemor Press self-publishing phase of Nin's career. Dennison reviews the background of Nin's small press publication in Paris and of her rejection by commercial houses that led to Nin's decision. She also provides material on Gonzalo More, Nin's companion in the publishing enterprise. Dennison pays particular attention to Nin's and More's attraction to the physical book as an art form.

My own "The Gemor Press" (also 1984) looks at a wider range of Gemor publications, attempting a comprehensive survey. I identify Nin's cousin, Eduardo Sanchez, as a third partner at least for the first Gemor publication. Descriptions of Gemor publications by Hugh Chisholm (including his translation of Paul Eluard's poetry), Sharon Vail, Berthie Zilkha, C. L. Baldwin, and Lee Ver Duft are provided along with brief biographical and bibliographical notes on these authors. This exploration makes it clear that Nin's Gemor Press was more than a self-publishing venture and attests to Nin's enormous entrepreneurial energy during the early and mid-forties.[2]

Secondary source bibliography has its first significant achievement in Rose Marie Cutting's *Anaïs Nin: A Reference Guide* (1978). Cutting's guide lists and annotates writings about Nin and her work beginning with Henry Miller's 1937 *Criterion* article on Nin's diary and ending with articles published some forty years later. Cutting divides the commentary for each year into two sections: one for books (including theses and dissertations), one for shorter writings. Within each section, the entries are listed alphabetically by author. Such demanding endeavors are rarely completely thorough or accurate, but Cutting's work – useful as it is – suffers from an abundance of omissions and errors. What is most puzzling is that she fails to include reviews and other items found in the notes and bibliographies to the critical studies already in print when her project was underway. One error, perhaps not representative, is naming me as author of the review of the *Anaïs Nin Reader* that appeared in *Choice*. How odd for an editor of a book to be asked to review it.

Cutting's work is supplemented by Richard R. Centing's "Writings About Anaïs Nin" updates that began appearing in *Pisces* 11.2 (Spring 1980) and continue through 12.3-4 (Summer/Fall 1981). The seventh such supplement appears in *Seahorse* 1.1 (1982) and the fourteenth and final supplement in *Seahorse* 2.4 (1983). Centing's annotations are always skillful, often playful, and sometimes catty. In "Updates and Amplifications," a regular feature of *Anaïs: An International Journal*, Gunther Stuhlmann often provides new information on writings about Nin.

Surveys of Criticism

Several brief overviews of Nin scholarship – some of them bibliographical essays – have preceded the present effort. Rose Marie Cutting, in the

"Introduction" to her reference guide (1978), discovers patterns in the mountain of comment she has annotated. In "Critical Approaches to Anaïs Nin" (1979), Margret Andersen patiently appraises the essays by various hands collected in Evelyn J. Hinz's *The World of Anaïs Nin* and reviews the orientation of Spencer's *Collage of Dreams*. She sets these studies and their presentations of Nin's vision against the feminist concerns of French writers Annie Leclerc and Hélène Cixous. Hinz's "Recent Nin Criticism: Who's on First?" (1982) is so stinging and ringing in its incisive attacks on the short-comings (as well as the motives) of Cutting, Spencer, Knapp, and Franklin/Schneider that the sensible, modulated passages of praise are overwhelmed. Gunther Stuhlmann's "What Did They Say? Writings about Anaïs Nin – An Informal Survey" (1983) takes students on a genial, ex-tremely readable, yet highly partisan journey. Barbara J. Griffin's "Two Ex-perimental Writers: Djuna Barnes and Anaïs Nin" (1983) offers a fair-minded and sensibly organized assessment. However, though otherwise rea-sonably thorough through 1979, Griffin ignores Hinz's important *The World of Anaïs Nin*, misses the significant challenges to Nin's stature by Frank Baldanza and Estelle Jelinek, and does not seem confidently grounded in the issues and primary texts. My own brief Nin entry in Beacham's *Research Guide to Biography and Criticism* (1985) provides capsule assessments of the major monographs and collections.

For Nin's reception abroad, see Marie-Claire Van Der Elst's "The Rec-ognition of AN in France: A Selective Bibliography" (1971), Catherine Broderick's "The Reception of Anaïs Nin in Japan" (1974), and Veronica Park Sagulo's "The Italian Response: How the Critics Dealt with Anaïs Nin's Work" (1988).

Biographical Studies

The fact that Nin chose to be her own biographer and to limit access to information on certain aspects of her life has handicapped biography and biographical criticism. Early biographical efforts, such as the anonymous sketch found in *Current Biography* (1944) and reprinted in Nin's pamphlet *Realism and Reality* (1946), are largely derived from information provided by Nin herself. Most of the biographical materials in reference books pro-vide little insight, and even the biographical passages in the major critical studies remain perfunctory. An outpouring of tributes followed Nin's death in 1977, many of them attempts at reading the meaning and message of her life. Sharon Spencer's "Anaïs Nin: A Heroine for Our Time" (1977) is among the most powerful. A more recent career study, one that emphasizes Nin's way of shaping her life creatively, is Vera John-Steiner's "From Life to Diary to Art in the Work of Anaïs Nin" (1989). Largely biographical in nature, this exploration attends to Nin's various writings as solutions to clearly defined artistic and personal problems. John-Steiner's attempts to trace "the development of Nin's methods of working, her way of thinking" (209), and she does so with reasonable success.

To the extent that Nin's *Diary*, a work in which she is the central character, has itself become a major object of study, it is difficult to drawn any clear line between understandings and assessments of her life and understandings and assessments of her life writing. Nevertheless, illuminating studies have appeared which, though dependent on Nin's *Diary*, on interviews, and on published and unpublished letters, take independent views of their subject.

Among those essays which consider Nin's relationships with other writers, four appear in Evelyn J. Hinz's *The World of Anaïs Nin: Critical and Cultural Perspectives* (1978). These are Ian S. MacNiven's "A Room in the House of Art: The Friendship of Anaïs Nin and Lawrence Durrell," Bernard F. Dick's "Anaïs Nin and Gore Vidal: A Study in Literary Incompatibility," Ekbert Faas's " 'The Barbaric Friendship with Robert [Duncan]': A Biographical Palimpsest," and my own "Doubles/Don Juans: Anaïs Nin and Otto Rank." Dick's study examines Nin's and Vidal's fictionalized portraits of one another, MacNiven's and Faas's reveal mutualities of influence, while my treatment of the Nin-Rank relationship stresses both the power of Rank's ideas on Nin's developing art and his disguised presences in her fiction. On the issue of doubles, it should be compared to Spencer's "The Dream of Twinship in the Writing of Anaïs Nin" mentioned below.

In the same spirit, but concerned with a more distant influence (one already treated comprehensively in Spencer's *Collage of Dreams*), is Frank S. Alberti's "Anaïs Nin, Reader of Proust: The Creative Affinities" (1979). In what may be called a partial biography of Nin's reading, Alberti traces the references to Proust in the *Diary* and elsewhere to argue that Nin not only found Proust's work nourishing as a model of artistic possibility, but that she also found the personage and the writing keys to understanding herself. Alberti notes that Leon Pierre-Quint's study of Proust was an aid to this understanding.[3] A similar enterprise is Julie A. Karsten's "Self-Realization and Intimacy: The Influence of D. H. Lawrence on Anaïs Nin" (1986). Karsten observes the key thematic parallels between the two writers as well as similarities in their uses of dreams, their methods of characterization, and their employment of cadenced prose. Affinities of life or career rather than art are at the center of Linde Salber's "Two Lives – One Experiment: Lou Andreas-Salomé and Anaïs Nin" (1991). Salber points out how both women struggled to define themselves in male-dominated environments and how neither was satisfied merely to test the limits and then withdraw. Psychoanalytic exploration and discovery was for Andreas-Salomé what writing was for Nin: a creative path to self-determination.

Sharon Spencer's "A Novel Triangle: Anaïs Nin – Henry Miller – Otto Rank" (1979) briefly explores the complex impact that these dynamic individuals had upon one another. Her more elaborate "Delivering the Woman Artist from the Silence of the Womb: Otto Rank's Influence on Anaïs Nin" (1982) is, like my own piece, more critical than biographical, stressing the full richness and complexity of Rank's ideas on creativity and feminine psychology rather than the attenuated versions found in Nin's *Diary*. A later essay by MacNiven, "Criticism and Personality: Lawrence Durrell – Anaïs Nin" (1984), measures the temperature of their relationship as friends and as writers. In "Years of Friendship: Correspondence with Caresse Crosby" (1984), Gunther Stuhlmann gathers and comments on key documents in that relationship. Patricia-Pia Célérier's "The Vision of Dr. Allendy: Psychoanalysis and the Quest for an Independent Identity" (1989) is a provocative discussion of Allendy's ideas, his stature, and his role in Nin's artistic and intellectual maturation. Célérier recounts various shortcomings in Allendy's handling of his difficult patient. Other biographical notes are available in various issues of *Pisces, Seahorse,* and *Anaïs.*

Biographical observations are also available in the form of Gunther Stuhlmann's prefaces to the seven volumes of *The Diary of Anaïs Nin* (1966-1980), Joaquin Nin-Culmell's prefaces to the four volumes of *The Early Diary of Anaïs Nin* (1978-1985), and Stuhlmann's introduction to his edition of Nin-Miller correspondence, *A Literate Passion* (1987). The impact of Paris on Nin's life and art is explored in J. Gerald Kennedy's "Place, Self, and Writing" (1990). When Nin returned to Paris as a young wife, her new experience of the city required a cognitive remapping. Kennedy traces what he considers a "curious relationship in which [Nin] had seemingly surrendered her will: the city in its various seasonal and meteorological aspects controlled her emotional life" (507). He shows how Nin remaps "the visible Paris in order to disclose an invisible world" (509).

Studies of Henry Miller invariably present views of Nin. Glimpses can be found in the Henry Miller chapter of George Wickes's *Americans in Paris, 1903-1939* (1969). Among all the full-length biographies of Miller, still valuable for its fairness, decorum, and color is the consideration of Nin in Jay Martin's *Always Merry and Bright: The Life of Henry Miller* (1978). More recent treatments include those found in Mary V. Dearborn's *The Happiest Man Alive: A Biography of Henry Miller*, in Robert Ferguson's *Henry Miller: A Life,* and in the chapter on Miller in John Tytell's *Passionate Lives* (all 1991). Ekbert Faas's *Young Robert Duncan: Portrait of the Poet As Homosexual in Society* (1983) incorporates and expands upon the treatment of the Nin-Duncan relationship found in his article listed above. The chapter on Nin in E. James Lieberman's *Acts of Will: The Life and Work of Otto Rank* (1985) intelligently surveys the available evidence and comments wisely on the Nin-Rank relationship but ends up raising more questions than it answers.

Nin's person looms large, for better and worse, in the memoirs of those whose lives were touched by hers in significant ways. Sometimes these memories are spurred by the occasion of reviewing *Diary* volumes, as is the case with Gore Vidal's satiric, patronizing "Taking a Grand Tour of Anaïs Nin's High Bohemia Via the Time Machine" (1971) in which Vidal attacks Nin's "contempt for intellect" and warns historians against trusting her facts. More affectionate are two remembrances by Kathleen Chase, "Anaïs Nin – Rumour and Reality: A Memoir" (1975) and "Being a 'Family' in France, 1930-1934" (1983), and Gilbert Culmell Chase's "From 'Kew' to Paris – A Personal Memoir" (1983). Far less attractive is the portrait painted by former friend and booster Maxwell Geismar in "Anaïs Nin: An Imprecise Spy in the House of Love" (1979). Geismar attacks the *Diary* volumes as pallid reconstructions of Nin's real work, and he attacks Nin for her self-promotional zeal. In two different pieces published in 1981, Gershon Legman tells the story of how Nin was commissioned to write pornography. Legman was the go-between.

Valuable for their exuberant affection are the three excerpts from Barbara Kraft's *Lux Aeterna Anaïs: A Memoir* that appear in the final issues of *Seahorse* in 1983 and Wayne McEvilly's curious blend of appreciation and reminiscence, "A Map of Music – Strange Dimensions of Politics and War" (1986). Fond recollections of Nin's supportive friendship flicker through Harold Norse's *Memoirs of a Bastard Angel* (1989).

Full-dress biographies are being prepared by Evelyn J. Hinz, Deidre Bair, and Noël Riley Fitch.[4]

General Assessments

Aside from the six book-length studies, there is a large body of shorter criticism that participates in the discussion of Nin's achievement from vantage points that cut across individual works and genres.

William Burford's "The Art of Anaïs Nin," first published in 1947 as an introduction to Nin's pamphlet titled *On Writing*, came at a crucial time in Nin's career. Dutton had just brought out her first two novels to mixed reviews, and Nin's own pamphlets of the mid-forties were battles in her war for understanding and recognition. Burford's comments are in tune with Nin's own arguments, but his prose style is more lucid in dealing with critical issues – no doubt because his mastery of the critical issues is more complete. He claims that critics judge Nin's writings by invoking standards and categories that are irrelevant to Nin's concerns and accomplishment, that they are blinded by older conventions of order that are not the conventions of Nin's developing art.

His attempt at clarifying Nin's ordering principle is not totally successful. Burford asserts, "The order which Anaïs Nin has perfected is the equality of literature and life." He continues, "The reader of her work feels that he is also the creator, that he has participated in a creative experience, in the destruction and the creation of her individuals" (43). Though Burford's elaboration of this thesis is attractive, few will accept a formulation that eliminates the boundary between art and life, while many will find quite different kinds of literary endeavors engaging them as participants in the creative experience. These readers will doubt that Nin has "created the true metaphor" that equates art and life. Useful as they are, Burford's formulations suffer from their unchecked enthusiasm. Moreover, his excessive establishment-bashing is not an effective strategy for winning people over.

Nonetheless, Burford's is the first prolonged discussion of Nin's aims and methods as a fiction writer by someone other than Nin herself. It sets in motion a special and unforeseen version of the dictum formulated by Alexander Pope in his "Essay on Criticism": "In ev'ry work regard the writer's end, / Since none can compass more than they intend." In the hands of Burford and later Nin advocates, Nin's reputation becomes unnecessarily connected with preciousness. By paying too much attention to her unique qualities and insisting that readers need a special education to enjoy her work, they tended to isolate her even while trying to build her audience. From the efforts of such friends Nin's reputation has never fully recovered.

Comprehensive discussions of Nin's work begin in 1962, made possible by the Swallow editions published the preceding year. For the first time, a substantial number of Nin's titles were in print simultaneously, though Nin's efforts as a diarist were still only legend. The publication of what appeared to be a "standard edition" of her writings carried a claim of importance to be tested by critical debate. The most notable of these early overviews are Oliver Evans's "Anaïs Nin and the Discovery of Inner Space," Frank Baldanza's "Anaïs Nin" (both 1962) and Harriet Zinnes's "Anaïs Nin's Works Reissued" (1963).

Evans tells of his early infatuation with Nin's work and his own attempt to write stories based on his understanding of Nin's theory of fiction. He then goes on to claim that an understanding of her theory is "indispensable for an appreciation of her work" (221), thus echoing Burford and setting the stage for a new generation of explainers while (no doubt unwittingly) suggesting that Nin's work is inaccessible to the uninitiated. Evans discusses Nin's concern with an individual's hidden layers of motive and the multiplicity of selfhood. He acknowledges that Nin's art has a specialized focus on characterization in which one central character is illuminated in relationship with "satellite selves" that revolve around it. Drawing illustrations from several of Nin's novels, Evans observes and applauds Nin's preference for the personal and subjective. He then examines several instances of Nin's two-fold method in representing the quest for self: "By directly presenting the reader with the symbols encountered in the character's dreams, daydreams, and fantasies; and by analyzing and interpreting these symbols through the methods of psychoanalysis" (226). Nin's technique, Evans asserts, including her employment of rhythmical language, aims for "the direct revelation of experience" (229) rather than a mere narration of events.

Baldanza's fault-finding essay, which appeared almost at the same time as Evans's accolade, matches it in intensity. He begins bluntly – "This is coterie writing" (263) – and then goes on to attack Nin's outlook and craft, leaving only one title ("Birth") unscorched. For Baldanza, Nin's narratives "are pointless, rambling explorations of erotic entanglements and neurotic fears in bohemian Paris, The Village, and Mexico, in which many of the same characters recur, nearly always haunted by an organ grinder playing airs from *Carmen*" (264). He deplores Nin's inability to manage coherent plots, her failure to develop a mature prose style, and her superficial rendering of relationships and of individuals' problems. Baldanza assumes that Nin's unwillingness to compromise with the established conventions of prose fiction is less a matter of rebellious genius than one of self-deceiving ineptitude. Between them, Evans and Baldanza formulate (or reformulate) the extremes of the debate over Nin's worth as a literary artist.

Harriet Zinnes's somewhat slighter piece is much more in tune with Evans's. Zinnes anticipates a wide audience for Nin with the appearance of the Swallow editions. Her discussion points out affinities between Nin's work and that of D. H. Lawrence, underscoring Nin's breaking of taboos, her passionate acceptance of all life has to offer, and her understanding of the predicament of modern woman. Zinnes is comfortable with the interiority of Nin's work, finding the motifs and methods of recurrence and flow both moving and meaningful. She finds Nin's ability to sustain a woman's vision "extraordinarily fresh in Anglo-American writing" (284), providing language and pattern both richly poetic and psychologically astute. Zinnes admits to failures by way of excess in some of Nin's writings (notably *House of Incest*), but on the whole finds Nin's work original and successful.

These essays, wider in focus than the individual items in the constant stream of review criticism, prepare the ground of issues developed in the six book-length monographs on Nin's work (released during the period 1968-1984) that follow the popular and critical success of her first published *Diary* volumes. The *Diary* volumes themselves present a new interest for critics, an interest that will be treated in a separate chapter. However, attempts at general assessments continue, spurred in part by the book-length discussions by Evans (1968) and Hinz (1971).

French students of American literature benefit from a reliable overview prepared by Pierre Brodin for his reference work *Vingt-Cinq Américains* (1969). This entry updates Brodin's entry of five years earlier (in *Présences Contemporaine: Écrivains Américains D'Aujourd'Hui*) by including comments on *Collages* and the *Diary*. Attentive to style and themes, Brodin's discussion makes the case for Nin's inclusion in a selective mapping of American writers at a time when American reference works did not grant her such distinction.

In "The Woman Writer and the Element of Destruction" (1972), Ellen Peck Killoh takes up the question of Nin's self-nomination as an artist and her attempt to break down the historical equation that connected the destructive element in the creative process to masculine qualities. Nin's struggle with stereotypes, reinforced (in part) by such authority figures as Rank, is one in which she sometimes succumbs, sometimes wins small but important victories. Killoh sets Nin's struggle in a historical and familial frame, then underscores her intention (stated in various ways in the *Diary* and elsewhere) of fashioning a constructive female art focused on connectedness. However, Killoh finds in Nin's fiction a repeated pattern of "missed connections"; her main characters manifest a longing for connection, but never achieve it. They do not even have vivid, deeply felt external conflicts. Avoiding confrontation (with its risk of destruction), they, like their creator, are driven to inward resolutions that leave them in isolation, if not in despair.

Anna Balakian's "The Poetic Reality of Anaïs Nin" (1973) is the most lucid exposition of Nin's esthetic in historical terms. Balakian finds Nin's work "related to two currents in European poetry" and the progression of her work can be paralleled to "the special conflict of philosophy and style that occurred in the passage from Symbolism to Surrealism" (116). Supporting her thesis with carefully selected passages that span Nin's career, Balakian draws instructive parallels to the outlook and method of André Breton, especially with regard to the handling of time and place. Balakian is also one of the first to accept (without anguishing over genre purity) the reciprocity of diary and fiction and the ultimate absence of a line between them. Nin was greatly impressed by Balakian's insights, successfully urging the inclusion of what was originally a formal paper as the introduction to the *Anaïs Nin Reader*. My own foreword to that anthology provides an overview of Nin's career, emphasizes her commitment to ideas, and characterizes the relationships among various Nin titles in "charting the ebbs and flows of the disturbed self moving toward psychic integration" (4).

Publication of the *Anaïs Nin Reader*, with its sampling of Nin's works in various genres, provided reviewers with a special opportunity to make general characterizations of Nin's work. The most important of these is Wallace Fowlie's *New York Times Book Review* piece in which the author summarizes Nin's themes and brings his Francophile expertise to bear on Nin's cultural inheritance. Also noteworthy are the responses by Nin stalwart Robert Kirsch ("Anaïs Nin's Literary Labyrinth"), novelist Marguerite Young, and Harriet Zinnes ("Reading Anaïs Nin").

In his "Anaïs Nin: Studies in the New Erotology" (1974), Orville Clark stresses another aspect of Nin's vision and esthetic. For Clark, Nin's *Diary* and her fiction have brought together "the joy of knowing and the joy of feeling . . . into one continuous stream of life and experience" (103). He sees Nin's achievement as one in which the ruinous traditional dichotomies in Western literature and culture have been reconciled. Echoing and embroidering upon Burford's view expressed nearly two decades earlier, Clark argues that Nin has bridged the gap between art and life as well as that between subjective and objective, unconscious and conscious, feeling and reason. In Nin's work, Clark finds the "sensuous body" to be the visible link between all the dichotomous pairings. He celebrates Nin as "a high priestess in the House of Erotica" (111) who is also a healer of souls.

Modest but engaging is Lynn Sukenick's "Anaïs Nin: The Novel of Vision" (1974), which, in spite of its title, really embraces all of Nin's fiction; indeed, all of her writing. Sukenick describes Nin's intuitive mode, her search for "a language of intuition" (158) and for a unified condition of the self. Like so many others (including Clark), Sukenick praises Nin's art as a healer's art, but she manages this task with brevity and taste.

A crucial exploration, the first systematic application of Rankian insights to a representative sampling of Nin's writings, is Sharon Spencer's "The Dream of Twinship in the Writings of Anaïs Nin" (1974-75). Even more than does Spencer's book-length study, this essay develops a compelling understanding of a Nin motif based on theories of her mentor. Spencer traces the appearances of this motif from *House of Incest* through the longer fictions and in the *Diary* as well, isolating four types of twinship and discovering the value of the "ideal of twinship" within Nin's major theme of the evolution of the self.

Two essays by Paul Grimley Kuntz claim our attention. The first, "Art as Public Dream: The Practice and Theory of Anaïs Nin" (1974), attends to Nin's interest in dreams and how they function in her writing. Kuntz sets side by side the *Diary* account of Nin's relationship to her father with the fictionalized version of these events in "Winter of Artifice" in order to elucidate the notion that art is the sharing of a dream. He also briefly explores Nin's critical writings, especially *The Novel of the Future*, to stress the originality of her discussion of dreams. Like Clark, Kuntz emphasizes a healing aspect of Nin's art, which he views as a kind of outward-reaching dream therapy.

Kuntz's second essay is "Anaïs Nin's 'Quest for Order' " (1978). Here he asserts the criteria of balance, harmony, and hierarchy in a reading of Nin which places her in touch with the tradition of St. Augustus and other "medieval Christian philosophers of the self" (211). Kuntz profitably discusses Nin's quarrel with Catholicism while maintaining that the quest for order that permeates her work is less secular than it is usually taken to be.

In her "Anaïs Nin: A Critical Evaluation" (1978), Estelle C. Jelinek provides one of those strongly negative assessments that appear with some regularity, providing a necessary if overstated counterbalance to the enthusiast tradition. Finding Nin's writings repetitious and her heroines unsympathetic, Jelinek satirizes Nin's career as a cult figure and questions the nature of her feminist stance. For Jelinek, "Nin's concept of woman is really an alternate form of sexism" (315); furthermore, her characters are still locked into finding their identity through men. Jelinek thinks that Nin's emphasis on the individual revolution is dubious, her impatience with group or social action destructive. All in all, Jelinek does not understand why so many women have been uncritically drawn to Nin's example. She finds Nin a weak spokesperson for the women's movement, largely ignorant of its history. For Jelinek and others, Nin's brand of feminism is not politically correct.

Less strident is the hybrid interview-discussion piece by Maxine Molyneux and Julia Casterton, "Looking Again at Anaïs Nin" (1982). Sensing that Nin is "a dissonant element" among prominent woman writers whose careers have raised issues regarding the tensions between writing and femininity, the authors are curious to probe the causes for Nin's problematic status among modern feminists. After a brief introduction by Casterton, the article provides Molyneux's previously unpublished 1970 interview with Nin, then a commentary by Casterton. Casterton is fascinated by what she sees as Nin's simultaneous desire to confess (whether in fiction or diary) and "to cover up the confession," thus producing a "delusive transparency" that Casterton connects to Nin's ambivalent stances toward the implied confessor (always male) and the institutions of power. Casterton views Nin's erotic writings, and more importantly her statements and silences about them, as lacunas in Nin's created personality, "an unintegrated part of Nin's public self" (100) that contributes to the dissonant note Nin rings in the feminist community.

Appreciations of how Nin's writing is influenced by and reflects her associations with the other arts occur frequently in the explications of individual works and in discussions of her style. Three articles make useful generalizations about such matters. In "Anaïs Nin and Music: Jazz" (1980), Kathleen Chase addresses the wide range of Nin's musical tastes and interests, her mixed affection for and rebellion against the classical inheritance of her formative years, and particularly her love for jazz. Chase states that Nin found in American jazz, with its improvisational character and its impressionistic response to life rhythms, an antidote to the esthetic of realism. Dolores Brandon's "Anaïs Nin, Sister to the Creators of Modern Dance" (1986) discusses attitudes that Nin shares with women who were leaders in modern dance. Brandon also reminds readers of how Nin uses dance as a recurrent motif in her writing, particularly as a metaphor for healing. Intriguing in its way, this essay reveals more about dance than it does about Nin. Robert A. Haller's brief "Anaïs Nin and Film: Open Questions" (1986) speculates on Nin's silences, reviews her connections with important filmmakers, and reminds us that there is more work to be done in this area.

One of the most peculiar discussions of Nin's work is found in Sharon Kubasak's "Doing the Limbo with Woolf and Nin: On Writer's Block" (1988). Kubasak ingeniously forces a reading of short story excerpts and a few *Diary* passages to uncover a description of the stages in writer's block.

Kubasak finds these observations that she attributes to Nin parallel to perceptions available in Woolf's *A Writer's Diary* and *To the Lighthouse*. Patricia M. Lawlor's "Beyond Gender and Genre – Writing the Labyrinth of the Self" (1989) examines the multiple meanings of the labyrinth as a "pivotal symbol" in all of Nin's work. It can represent the unknown, the unconscious, and the myth-making process. Lawlor pays special attention to the story called "The Labyrinth," but refers to Nin's *Diary*, her other fiction, and her critical prose as well.

Among the more recent overviews of Nin's career and achievement is Sharon Spencer's fine offering "The Music of the Womb: Anaïs Nin's 'Feminine' Writing" (1989). Spencer argues that Nin is a radical writer in three ways. First, she writes on such tabooed subjects as incestuous longing, lesbianism, and love affairs between socially inappropriate partners. Next, she breaks away from genre conventions to develop autonomous forms. Finally, she develops a musicality of style and structure. Spencer explores each of these characteristics, which she connects with the 'feminine' quality in Nin's work, by examining both the earlier and later fiction, all the while applauding Nin's courage as an ardent experimenter. A companion essay that strikes many of the same general chords, though perhaps better characterized as career biography than analysis, is Spencer's "The Feminine Self: Anaïs Nin" (1990).

Hoshang Merchant, in "Out of and into the Labyrinth: Approaching the Aesthetics of Anaïs Nin" (1990), reviews old ground in discussing how Nin's art derives from her interest in symbolism, surrealism, and psychoanalysis. Merchant stresses Nin's search for a "polyvalent" poetic language that brings pleasure through its resonances and overtones. He also observes her conscious avoidance of such structural clichés as epiphanic or tragic conclusions; Nin's forms, like life itself, are tentative.

Two overlapping bio-critical studies are Ellen G. Friedman's reference article "Anaïs Nin" (1991) and her "Escaping from the House of Incest: On Anaïs Nin's Efforts to Overcome Patriarchal Constraints" (1992). The former, though riddled with the kind of bibliographical errors that damage its reference reliability, is an effective overview of Nin's life and art that stresses dominant themes while touching upon Nin's major works in various genre. The heart of its interpretive thrust is also found in the latter essay in which Friedman convincingly argues that "incest in Nin's works speaks not only to woman's relationship to man but also to the woman artist's relationship to traditional forms of expression and to the patriarchy in general" (39). Reviewing *Diary* material, *House of Incest*, and the *Winter of Artifice* stories, Friedman finds the bases of Nin's rebellion against a male definition of a woman writer. Nin "redefined the category" and thus freed herself from "incestuous literary practices" (45).

Bertrand Mathieu's "On the Trail of Eurydice" (1992) is part of the prospectus for a book-length study of Nin's work. Mathieu reviews the standard interpretation of the myth of Orpheus and Euridice, a perspective that judges Euridice an appropriate sacrifice to Orpheus's (man's) art. For Mathieu, Nin reverses the myth by playing both parts: she is Orpheus to her own Euridice. Other sections of his discussion examine Nin's use of dreams and her special, intuitive brand of Gnosticism.

In "Anaïs Nin and the Developmental Use of the Creative Process" (1992), Susan Kavaler-Adler explores most of Nin's fictional texts to show how Nin's work "demonstrates the resolution of a narcissistic neurosis" in a case in which "traumatic loss of a father [interferes] with the potential maturational resolution of such narcissistic yearnings that become focused on the father" (73). Most of the discussion draws upon "Winter of Artifice," but *House of Incest*, *A Spy in the House of Love*, and *Collages* also receive significant attention. Through her art, Kavaler-Adler concludes, "Nin transcends retaliation" (87).

Notes to Chapter 2

[1]A warm-up for Franklin's Nin bibliography is his article "AN's Recordings, Editorship of Periodicals, and Films" (1971). Of related interest is Franklin's "AN and the Rare Book Trade" (1972), an overview of rare editions and the marketplace.

[2]Of related interest is my "Oscar Baradinsky's 'Outcasts': Henry Miller, Anaïs Nin, Maya Deren and The Alicat Book Shop Press" (1985).

[3]For more on this matter, see Gunther Stuhlmann's "Léon Pierre-Quint: Mastering the Art of Marcel Proust" (1988) and Edouard Roditi's "On Proust and Pierre-Quint" (1989).

[4]Though arguably not biography, students still need to know about Robert Snyder's documentary film, *Anaïs Observed* (1973) and the book derived from it, *Anaïs Nin Observed* (1976). Unclassifiable but mixing biography, praise, and the spirit of a happening is *Celebration with Anaïs Nin*, edited by Valerie Harms (1973).

3: Nin's Critical Prose

AS A GROUP, Nin's critical writings have received little attention. Primarily explanations and justifications of her own practice, they attract the attention of Nin specialists while remaining ignored by most other readers – even those concerned with critical theory. Indeed, aside from review criticism and the obligatory coverage found in the book-length treatments of Nin's work, only one other significant discussion is available, and that is Patricia A. Deduck's *Realism, Reality, and the Fictional Theory of Alain Robbe-Grillet and Anaïs Nin* (1982).

Nin's first book, *D. H. Lawrence: An Unprofessional Study* (1932), appeared in a limited edition and received limited attention. In a patronizing and revoltingly sexist review, Waverley Root considers Nin's discussion of Lawrence pretty good for woman's work but severely limited by the gender of the author. Nin, Root claims, can lay out some of the pieces of Lawrence's achievement but cannot find the overriding unity. He makes a special point of stressing Nin's over-reliance on Lawrence's psychological studies as bases for approaching Lawrence's art. How ironic that Nin would be accused of falling into the same kind of trap that her own critics would in turn be accused of falling into.

Also rather dismissive is the brief comment of the *Times Literary Supplement* reviewer found in the omnibus review "D. H. Lawrence in Retrospect." The reviewer finds Nin only too appreciative and her prose "staccato"; nevertheless, there is praise for Nin's approach to Lawrence's characters and to his use of dreams and fantasy.[1]

The book was more or less ignored until the Swallow edition appeared in 1964 sporting an introduction by Harry T. Moore. Setting Nin's book in the context of early Lawrence criticism, Moore finds it a remarkable achievement for its time, and he repeats his praise (first made in his 1951 *The Life and Works of D. H. Lawrence*) for Nin's discussion of the texture of Lawrence's work. Emphasizing the young Nin's "emotional knowledge," Moore believes that the book on Lawrence marks her own passage from girlhood to young womanhood (a delayed transition if he is correct). A number of reviews respond to this first American edition, perhaps the most detailed and generally enthusiastic being found in Paul West's "D. H. Lawrence: Mystical Critic" (1965), an omnibus review of Lawrence criticism. While alert to Nin's errors and probable misjudgments, West praises Nin's discussion of Lawrence's Englishness, his view of male comradeship, and his affinity with Whitman. West also admires the way in which Nin's book captures the impact Lawrence can have on an individual sensibility.

Oliver Evans excuses himself from assessing this and Nin's other critical efforts in his 1968 *Anaïs Nin* by claiming that his book "was conceived as criticism rather than criticism of criticism" (xvii). Clearly, however, his discussions of Nin's stories and novels are informed by a knowledge of this early effort, and Evans quotes from both *Realism and Reality* and *On Writing*.

With her study of 1971, Evelyn J. Hinz brings Nin's critical writings the sophisticated, sympathetic understanding they had never previously received. In fact, Hinz's analysis of Nin's two book-length critical works (each receiving a chapter) comprises fully twenty-five percent of her discussion. This balance (or imbalance) marks Hinz as the critic most helpful in providing Nin's own critical orientation as the major key to understanding her achievement as fiction writer and diarist.

Despite its understated title – "A Word About Influences and Unprofessional Studies" – Hinz's chapter on the Lawrence book is a carefully constructed effort to redirect conventional expectations. Admitting that Nin's "interpretation of Lawrence's art and her terminology are critically inadequate" (17) by conventional standards, Hinz argues that Nin's book is a new kind of creative criticism that is still valuable in many ways. Nin does not fail in an exercise of objective criticism, but succeeds in expressing a subjective criticism that is true to the intuitive and poetic way of knowing that she finds in Lawrence. Furthermore, Hinz points out that Nin's criticism is to a large measure influenced by Lawrence's own criticism, and that both writers produce a criticism that is simultaneously art.

Hinz attends to the structure of Nin's study and to its overarching concern with the problem of perception. She argues that Nin is not so much concerned with explicating Lawrence as she is with responding to Lawrence in a way that advances her evolving, personal esthetic. Many of Nin's responses, then, are especially helpful as keys to the fictions she has yet to write; only occasionally and secondarily are they valuable as keys to Lawrence's work. Thus, for Hinz, *Lawrence* is Nin's first creative book from which her later writings develop. It is not even, as it is often taken to be, important as testimony to the power of Lawrence's influence on Nin. That is, reading Lawrence will not help us find Nin as much as reading Nin will. Better versed in Lawrence's writings than most Nin critics, Hinz was perfectly positioned to value Nin's first book for what it is and to warn against measuring it by assuming intentions Nin never had.

Spencer does not concern herself with Nin's first book, but Bettina L. Knapp's *Anaïs Nin* (1978) includes a chapter titled "Creative Criticism – *D. H. Lawrence: An Unprofessional Study*" in which Knapp echoes much of what Hinz establishes. However, Knapp catches both Lawrence and Nin in a network of allusions to representative European thinkers on personality, knowing, perception, and expression that enriches the quest after Nin's theoretical stance. Dividing her discussion into four subsections, Knapp probes Nin's reflections on intuition, dreams, and symbols as literary vehicles and ways of knowing. Most striking is Knapp's subsection on synesthesia. Here, Knapp argues that for Nin synesthesia is not merely a literary device but a mystical awakening. The "synesthetic experience" requires a "dissociation of ego" that allows one to experience the range of sense impressions simultaneously (27). According to Knapp, Nin finds in Lawrence both the understanding and example of creative processes that enabled the artist to make the unknown known, to render the amorphous palpable. Even more than Hinz's, Knapp's discussion of Nin's creative criticism reveals a spiritual dimension or aura. Invoking Bergson, the French symbolists, and various neo-Platonists, Knapp's somewhat exotic exploration imagines a Nin whose immersion in Lawrence liberated and transformed her, finally delivering her not into Lawrence's shadow but to herself.

Franklin and Schneider (1979) treat the Lawrence study briefly in a short chapter that examines it along with *The Novel of the Future*. These critics tend to take Nin's title at face value; they summarize its main points while valuing the book for the writerly insights of a young and untrained apprentice in fiction. Calling Nin's technique "a modified explication de texte" (270), Franklin and Schneider observe two broad divisions: a discussion of Lawrence's themes and an analysis of key works. They appreciate Nin's directness and focus, but at the same time judge the book among Nin's lesser efforts. For these critics, Nin fails to provide sufficient contextualizing background and takes a disturbingly narrow approach. Without quite saying so, Franklin and Schneider implicitly refute the stance taken by Hinz and Knapp. They do not find Nin's subjective approach a virtue, and they certainly do not consider her study of Lawrence representative of a new kind of creative criticism.

Scholar (1984) mentions *Lawrence* in her discussion of "Major Influences." She praises it as a successful defense of Lawrence and quickly lists those aspects of Lawrence's vision and technique that had an impact on Nin's own work, both for better and for worse.

Thus, of the critics who fashioned the six book-length studies of Nin's work, only two consider it important enough to warrant extended treatment.[2]

Nin's pamphlet essays of the 1940s, *Realism and Reality* (1946) and *On Writing* (1947), receive passing attention by Hinz (along with Nin's 1959 essay "The Writer and the Symbols"). However, neither she nor the other major critics give these interim documents systematic attention. They are slight, and there is really no need to consider them in detail. My own discussion of their import and occasion, "A Delicate Battle Cry – Anaïs Nin's Pamphlets of the Forties" (1990), appears in an issue of *Anaïs: An International Journal* in which the essays themselves are reprinted. They are best thought of as preliminaries to Nin's elaborate discussion of her principles and practice, *The Novel of the Future* (1968), and they are treated as such by Deduck and others.

As might be expected, this study was praised by Nin partisans and damned by her detractors. However, some felt that Nin damaged her own reputation as a significant diarist and fiction writer by attempting to enter a field in which she had no competence. Such is the stance of Florence Casey's "A Bird Does not Need to Study Aviation." Among the put-downs is the anonymous *Times Literary Supplement* piece called "Herself Surprised" that finds Nin patronizing and out of her depth. Positive responses include those by Granville Hicks in *Saturday Review* and Bettina Knapp in *The Village Voice.* One of the more detailed responses is Miriam Waddington's "Review of Anaïs Nin's *The Novel of the Future.*" Waddington praises Nin's courage in discussing the novel "through image and illustration instead of through critical argument" (55). While admitting that Nin underestimates the importance of economic and other factors, Waddington provides a fine summary and appreciation of Nin's intent and of the value of her approach.

In her chapter "Backward and Forward," Evelyn J. Hinz offers the second most elaborate discussion of *Novel.* Comparing it to Nin's Lawrence book and to her other early critical formulations, Hinz observes that *Novel* employs a more logical structure. Hinz also finds Nin being negative and defensive while in the Lawrence book she was on the offense. However, these differences in stance and tone, Hinz maintains, should not obscure a consistency in vision. In *Novel* Nin gives fuller elaboration and more copious illustration to the key ideas and terms in her critical perspective. In so doing, she also sets herself in contemporary literary history. Hinz summarizes Nin's comments on neurosis, drugs, pop art, and other issues while stressing Nin's concern with maintaining the validity of her career-long struggle against the realist tradition.

Franklin and Schneider emphasize the limited focus of Nin's book. Despite its title, *Novel* is "a loosely organized analysis of her own writing . . . along with introductions of other writers when their works illustrate an attempt or approach that Nin wished to emphasize" (273). Nin has neither the critical tools nor the historical perspective to accomplish more than this. The book is both a rationale for Nin's own practice and a retrospective view of how she discovered and developed her characteristic techniques. As they summarize Nin's arguments and topics, Franklin and Schneider find the book thematically coherent but less forceful and less lucid on its major concerns than related passages in the fiction and in the *Diary.*

In her *Realism, Reality, and the Fictional Theory of Alain Robbe-Grillet and Anaïs Nin* (1982), Patricia A. Deduck performs an extended comparison of *Novel* and Robbe-Grillet's *Pour un Nouveau Roman* (1963). This comparison is elaborated and its major insights repeated far beyond the boundaries of necessity, no doubt to bulk up to the minimum requirement for a doctoral dissertation. Nonetheless, it is readable and instructive.

Both Robbe-Grillet and Nin share a concern with establishing a critical perspective that goes beyond a mere defense of their own practices. Both also argue for fluidity in genre definition; they opt for change and growth rather than the fixity that is the equivalent of death. Art must continue to change because man continues to evolve.

More vital similarities have to do with a shared notion that understandings of what constitutes reality are crucial to both the evolution of the human spirit and the fictional writings that express it. Both writers reject inherited mimetic schemes, literary realism in particular, in that such schemes tend toward a rigidity that forestalls discovery. Each author defines the novel as a means of exploration, as a form of research rather than the result of research. Furthermore, according to Deduck, both Robbe-Grillet and Nin reject the idea that "reality" and "truth" are equivalent terms. They "view reality, essentially, as product of imagination and realism" (66). Thus the artwork is a search for and creation of reality, not a representation of it. In this spirit, each views the novel as a continuous form – as open-ended as the notion of quest or the process of evolution. Finally, then, Deduck is determined to underscore her belief that the shared esthetic of Nin and Robbe-Grillet envisions the coming together of art and life.

Though critics often make reference to Nin's occasional pieces collected in *A Woman Speaks* (1975) and *In Favor of the Sensitive Man* (1976), only Franklin and Schneider have assessed them as part of the Nin canon. They suggest that these books could have only come into being in the afterglow of Nin's celebrity, and that neither offers much in the way of critical insight, literary polish, or new information – though each offers a bit.

Notes to Chapter 3

[1]Some thirty years later, another *TLS* review, "Private View," gives more enthusiastic attention to the first English edition of 1961.

[2]For a discussion of Lawrence's appeal to "proto-feminists" including Nin, see Sandra M. Gilbert's "Feminism and D. H. Lawrence" (1991).

4: Nin's Shorter Fiction

House of Incest

NIN'S FIRST PUBLISHED BOOK of fiction was *House of Incest* (1936), and for
many of her readers this early effort shows her at her best. There is a
strong consensus that the major themes that will occupy Nin throughout
her career are found in embryonic form in this lush prose poem. Though it
would be decades until Nin's emergence from obscurity produced a body of
significant criticism on this title, a number of early responses should be
noted, even though only two appeared in print at the time.

By the spring of 1931, Nin had begun the experimentation that would
eventually lead to *House*. By 1932, Henry Miller had seen the evolving
work, and in a letter of 1933 (published in 1944 as "Letter to Anaïs Nin Regarding One of Her Books") Miller rhapsodizes over material that would
be transformed into *House* passages. By 1934, Nin would be showing it to
her analyst, Otto Rank. Both men had a strong influence on Nin as she
pursued her self-awareness as a woman and her development as an artist.
The final version of *House* is certainly Nin's own, but it is also the result of
responding to the opinions of these two mentors, one a lover and the other
a would-be lover.

By late 1934, Rank had prepared a preface for the work (just as Nin had
produced one for Miller's *Tropic of Cancer*). His reference to "Mandra," a
name that does not exist in any of the published editions, shows that he was
reacting to a version of the prose poem that continued to evolve after his
exploration. Rank's writing here exhibits a proprietary interest in the prose
poem (which he offered to publish) and a possessive interest in Nin. Alraune (transformed into Sabina in the final version), Rank tells us, is "the
symbol of the bad woman as conceived by bewitched man who felt
threatened by sexual destruction . . . here recreated by a woman who was
made bad by her father and who first wanted to win him back by becoming
good. When this failed she became bad again, this time not only to please
him – because he wanted her bad – but also to punish him with her badness"
(51-52). Rank continues to explore the work's evocation of woman's possible destinies in a world fashioned and dominated by male values and
visions. He is not at all conscious of his own imposition and his own self-
portrait as a surrogate father. He has nothing to say, because it has nothing
to do with him, about the work's style or structure.

Nin's claim that Rank not only pressed her to finish *House* but also
helped her understand it (*Diary* 2: 31) and her rendering of a scene in which
he exhibits his smothering excitement over a passage (*Diary* 2: 38-39) illus-

trate Rank's lack of objectivity. The preface itself does the rest. Clearly, Rank's observations quoted above come at least as much from his privileged (professional) insights into Nin's past and then-current dilemma with her father as they do from his researches into the psychodynamics of myth.

Rank's preface is important, however, in that it articulates an understanding that *House* introduces and that Nin's later works elaborate: "The fundamental lie, the real falsification of nature is – as all spiritual creation – the man's, who first usurps all creation and then creates the woman – whose creature he is – out of his rib or his brain in order to blame and to punish her for what she has become through him" (54). Nin alternately accepts (as an explanation for female suffering) and strives to undermine and replace this tradition throughout her career.

Rank's was not the only bit of front matter provided to help stimulate publication of *House*. A brief piece by Nin friend and James Joyce expert Stuart Gilbert also survives (not published in full until included in Zaller's *Casebook*), designated a foreword, which draws attention to Nin's daring evocation of passion, the place of imagination and projection, the fine balance "between self-abandon and analysis," and the poetic qualities of the book (1). This appreciation parallels a review by Gilbert ("Passion in Parenthesis") published in the periodical *Reading and Collecting*. The review carries the publication information "Privately Printed for the Author, 1937. $7.50." Such intriguing information suggests either that Gilbert had prepared the review before Nin worked out the publisher's imprint or that another printing (or edition) followed the 1936 Siana edition.

A third early response by way of foreword is by Miller himself, who with Nin and Michael Fraenkel formed Siana Editions to get their works (including *House*) into print. This appreciation, and a shorter version of it slated to be a review, addresses a two-part book divided by settings and motifs of night and day. Miller, like Rank, was no doubt reacting to an early draft. Yet he does comment vividly on the motif of birth and becoming and on Nin's evocative power and risk-taking. Finally, though, the essay tells us more about Miller's infatuated bravado than about Nin's writing.

Another Miller offering is not a piece of criticism but rather a creative work called "Scenario," parenthetically subtitled "A Film With Sound," which Miller says "is directly inspired by a phantasy called *The House of Incest* written by Anaïs Nin" (*Cosmological Eye* 75). This piece was first published in a limited edition (Paris: Obelisk Press, 1937). From the Miller/Nin correspondence (*A Literate Passion*), we can tell that "Scenario" existed in some form as early as December 1934 when Miller offered it as a Christmas gift to Nin (262) and as testimony to how well he knew the work – implying, of course, his intimacy with Nin (288). In orchestrating a surreal pageant of courtship between Alraune and Mandra, Miller emphasizes the lesbian aspect of the relationship in *House*, an aspect that Rank also notes. Though this work cannot be assessed as criticism, all students of the Nin-Miller relationship should be aware of this intuitively rich response to Nin's earliest creative effort.

For all the enthusiasm and promotional zeal, the first edition of *House* had a tiny print run that did not get far beyond Nin's immediate circle. The book occasioned mostly silence for the next thirty years – even when, capitalizing on the momentum of her recent success with a commercial publisher, E. P. Dutton, Nin issued a new edition of *House* from Gemor Press in mid 1947. However, while earlier Gemor publications had received useful reviews, this newly available edition of her first work did not benefit from the attention paid to those or to the Dutton releases of *Ladders to Fire* and *Children of the Albatross*. Its appearance as part of the English edition of *Under a Glass Bell* (1947) caused no stir. At the close of 1958 Nin self-published the work again, but it received only sketchy, scattered mention – most of it due to Nin's association with the bilingual journal *Two Cities*. When Nin's older works were reprinted and her new titles published by Swallow, beginning in 1961, most of the attention was given to *Seduction of the Minotaur* and the collected *Cities of the Interior*. Not until the first book-length study of her work, Oliver Evans's *Anaïs Nin* (1968), did *House* receive anything more than a passing mention.

Evans devotes almost ten percent of his study to Nin's first and slightest separate title, thereby underscoring its centrality. He establishes its associative method, examines the contributions of each of its several "movements," and discovers two symbolic levels of meaning attached to the surrealistic imagery and action.

In Evans's analysis, the first movement, or prologue, concerns itself with birth both on a personal level and that of the collective unconscious. The second and longest movement dramatizes the theme of self-love in the form of homoerotic love. The third movement constitutes a withdrawal based on the recognition of this false love's failure and its cause. But isolation is no relief. The same prison of self-love is the thematic burden of the fourth, fifth, and sixth movements, though now the terms are literally incestuous – a brother and sister relationship. The seventh and final movement, in Evans's analysis, is the narrator's relationship with her work (her writing as self-creation), which is finally understood as yet another version of unhealthy narcissism. In the final pages, the reader is brought to three exhibits, "extremes of psychological anguish whose source is self-obsession" (42). One character is paralyzed by unattainable goals, another by hypersensitivity, and another by possessiveness. In each case, Evans shows how Nin renders the psychological state through suggestive imagery. He observes that the suffering of each unfulfilled character in *House* is intensified by the degree of self-knowledge each possesses.

In dealing plainly and precisely with the genesis of the work, its place in the Nin canon, and its methods and meanings, Evans sets the discussion of *House* on a high plateau. He establishes useful frames of reference to familiar authors (Faulkner, Emerson, Poe) as well as to more immediate inspirations (Mirbeau, Lautréamont, Rimbaud). He makes plausible sense of the work's difficulties, reveals its kind of unity and coherence, warns against temptations toward misreadings, and avoids extravagant praise. He would be a difficult act to follow.[1]

The book-length studies by Evelyn J. Hinz and Sharon Spencer that follow in 1971 and 1977 are not organized by works and pay only passing attention to *House*. However, in her 1978 *Anaïs Nin*, Bettina L. Knapp provides a thirty-page chapter that elaborates useful contexts for understanding the unusual nature of Nin's achievement. Knapp begins with a thumbnail sketch of surrealism, observing that Nin shared the surrealists' "longing for the marvelous and the fantastic and their belief in the unconscious as a storehouse of riches" (39). Knapp is careful not to overstate the affinities and influence of this movement on Nin, and she states Nin's divergence from surrealist credo as well as her indebtedness to the ideas and practices of Breton, Artaud, and others.

Knapp's other contribution is to describe the way in which *House* emerged from a therapeutic process in which Nin was then deeply engaged, first with René Allendy and then with Otto Rank. She asserts: "*House of Incest* was the outcome in large measure of Nin the patient and the psychotherapeutic sessions working in conjunction with Nin the artist" (44). After sketching Nin's relationship with each man and outlining what she drew from each, Knapp attends to the creative process as it both surrounds and is embedded in the book. She argues that the metaphor of birth with which *House* begins is directed not just at artistic self-creation, but at the pain of separation. The necessary pain of giving birth to the book is, then, in large measure what the book expresses. With it, Nin transforms herself into an artist.

Knapp's discussions of lesbianism, incest, and narcissism take a somewhat different direction from Evans's, stemming as they do from the fairly detailed and specialized contexts Knapp provides. However, the essential understandings derived from these discussions are close enough to those of Evans not to demand separate elaboration. What is strikingly original, though not altogether convincing, is Knapp's treatment of *House* as "An Alchemical Drama" (many have noted the alchemical symbols used as section dividers). After reviewing the way in which Nin's interest in alchemy derived from her relationship with Dr. Allendy, Knapp asserts, "As the alchemist performs his transmutations, so the protagonists in *House of Incest* intuit their way through the seven chapters of the prose poem: the seven hells or heavens of the creative process, the seven days of Creation" (60).

Knapp examines the ways in which the alchemical stages of "nigredo," "albedo," and "rubedo" are manifest in Nin's narration and imagery. The stage of blackness, of chaos and death, is the primordial (or prenatal) condition with which the book begins. Within it, "the seed of creation or of transformation is implanted" (61). The "albedo" or white stage is a period of purification and initiation. In the final phase, "rubedo" or redness, the alchemist's fire transforms – as does the fire of passion and insight. Knapp's application of this frame of reference is imaginative and challenging. Its great advantage is that it provides Knapp with an organizing principle within which she can attend to Nin's image-laden, luxuriant diction.

Knapp asks us to understand *House* as Nin's transformation, her breakthrough, that made the rest of her career as an artist possible.

A curious side note to the commentary on *House* is Ian Hugo's brief memoir, "The Making of *Bells of Atlantis*," in which the engraver and filmmaker recalls the transformation of his wife's prose poem (which he considers "her most inspired work"). The interaction of images in the original is paralleled in the film by "sandwich printing," an early version of superimposition. Like Nin, Hugo testifies to his faith in approaches to art that allow unconscious elements to emerge. Like Miller's "Scenario," Hugo's *Bells of Atlantis* underscores the sensory dimension of Nin's language in *House*, and also like "Scenario" the film may be called an interpretation of Nin's original work. (The film, in which Nin appears, was completed in 1952.)

In their *Anaïs Nin: An Introduction* (1979), Benjamin Franklin V and Duane Schneider plunge readers into an opening chapter on *House*, making it serve in place of a formal introduction to their study. Franklin and Schneider make the most emphatic evaluative statement: *House* is Nin's "first, best, and most challenging volume of prose fiction" (4). Their task, conducted with skill and authority, is to defend that assertion, which they do in a number of ways. Most importantly, they demonstrate how in this work Nin developed the most effective relationship of style and content.

Because their discussion of this work serves as an introduction to the rest of Nin's writings, the authors pursue an understanding of what, for Nin, is the essential nature of reality and the proper (because healthiest) attitude toward it. They demonstrate how *House* reflects Nin's concern with a balanced perspective in which objective reality is acknowledged but not allowed to stifle or dominate the equally important dream life. *House*, however, more than Nin's other works, dramatizes the "dangers of living too exclusively in the dream state" (7). In a step by step examination, Franklin and Schneider address Nin's key themes and techniques, stressing the issue – that is both theme and technique – of wholeness versus multiplicity.

Franklin and Schneider note particular problems in Nin's text. One of these is the difficulty, most pronounced in the section dealing with Jeanne and in the penultimate paragraph, of identifying speakers. In the case of the Jeanne section, this difficulty is resolved by means of a chart identifying the speakers paragraph by paragraph. Just as useful, however, is the observation that certain distinctions are perhaps unimportant or left intentionally ambiguous since the overall work involves fusion of fragments and reconciliation of opposites. All voices, that is, are aspects of a diffused consciousness. This chapter is certainly one of the best close readings of *House*, and it is also among the most accessible. While insisting that this work "demands the full attention of the reader" (19), Franklin and Schneider do an admirable job of keeping the reader in mind.

In his "Anaïs Nin" entry for the *DLB* volume on *Americans Writers in Paris, 1920-1939* (1980), Franklin covers some of this same ground as he traces the early stages of Nin's growth as a writer in the context of the nourishing Parisian artistic culture.

The next extended discussion of *House* is Nancy Scholar's chapter, "*House of Incest*: Through a Glass Darkly," in her *Anaïs Nin* (1984). Of all critics to date, Scholar most firmly sets this piece, as well as Nin's entire body of work, in the female literary tradition as defined by such critics as Elaine Showalter, Sandra Gilbert, and Susan Gubar. Viewing the work as a representative (while still unique) female text opens up possibilities for emphasis and understanding not available in earlier treatments. Here is a typical passage:

> In keeping with the traditional framework of woman's existence, *House* is a completely hermetic work: air-tight and claustrophobic in the extreme. Virtually all the action takes place within the woman's realm: the house. (72)

Though more subdued in her praise of the prose poem than Franklin and Schneider, Scholar also considers it Nin's most successful fiction (though for Scholar Nin's fiction takes a distant second place to the *Diary*). Before beginning her detailed analysis, Scholar pays attention to the influence (or inspiration) of Rimbaud, C. J. Jung, and Rank. She also sketches something of Miller's role in the composition of *House*.

Scholar then treats the divisions of the book under separate headings: parts one, two, three, and seven separately; parts four, five, and six together (as "Inside the House of Incest"). She singles out the second section, with its handling of "the universal drama of the double," as an example of Nin's best writing, while recognizing its roots in the *Diary* 1 portrait of June Miller. For Scholar, Nin's "most inspired writing . . . describes the sensation of self-division" (81). Throughout her analysis, Scholar's allusions – to Sylvia Plath's *The Bell Jar* and "Lady Lazarus," to Charlotte Bronte's *Jane Eyre*, to Doris Lessing's *Golden Notebook* – sustain her various individual points and her general orientation regarding *House* and female literary tradition.

As her chapter title suggests, Scholar also develops a connection between Nin's work and the films of Ingmar Bergman. Though she leaves much to the reader regarding *Through a Glass Darkly*, Scholar establishes a firm connection between the prose poems and a scene in Bergman's *Persona*. Passing references to other films, like Fellini's *Juliet of the Spirits*, attest once again to the cinematic quality of Nin's poetic prose. As have others, Scholar remarks that the book concludes with a sense of direction, but no clear resolution.

In a separate piece first published in 1979 and reprinted in Spencer's anthology (1986), "Anaïs Nin's *House of Incest* and Ingmar Bergman's *Persona*: Two Variations on a Theme," Scholar develops the Nin-Bergman affinity ("congruence") more effectively. Both works, she asserts, distill career-long obsessional themes, both aspire to wordless communication, and both involve dream states. More importantly, the works are linked by their reflection of Jung's concept of shadow and persona. Scholar examines the important parallels in the exploration of doubling and the shadow self. In each, the moment of total identification is the dramatic center. Scholar's parallels promote interesting emphases, but provide no new readings.

Gary Sayre's "*House of Incest*: Two Interpretations" (also in Spencer) does not so much break new ground as it clarifies themes and methods. Sayre offers that incest "signifies any form of self-love which is essentially selfish, or ego-oriented" (47), thus excusing Nin for a seemingly misleading title since literal incest occupies only a portion of the book. In the narrator and each of the other characters, this incestuous longing holds a "peculiar self-contradiction [that] spells out certain destruction" (50). Sayre's second "interpretation" investigates "the dialectical marriage of dream and reality" that gives birth to the work of art. The dichotomy that must be made constructive is figured in many ways, including the opposition of body and mind. Sayre does not really have "two interpretations," but relatively isolated treatments of two themes.

In her *Women of the Left Bank* (1986), Shari Benstock sketches Nin's early career before comparing *House* to Djuna Barnes's *Nightwood*. She sees these works as having parallel subject matter and imagery. Benstock believes that the degree of emotional distress in *House* and other early Nin titles reflects the deep malaise in European culture during the 1930s: "The psychopathology of the female spirit that is the subject of her writing in these years reflects a larger cultural paranoia and self-hatred" (435).

In "Interaction and Cross-Fertilization" (1986), Valerie Harms discusses the specific ways in which Henry Miller influenced Nin's early fiction, including *House*. However, she draws details from the manuscript of an unpublished, apprentice novel which contains Miller's comments and corrections. More to the point is her "The Dream Is the Key–The Drafts That Became *House of Incest*" (1987) in which Harms comments on the development of the prose poem from manuscript drafts (held at Northwestern University) that contain the seminal dreams. At one time, the characters in Nin's developing book were called Alraune I, Alraune II, and Alraune III. Harms's study is truly illuminating, providing a fascinating view of Nin's struggle with her developing art and of the creative process itself.

Finally, in "The Genesis of 'Alraune'–Some Notes on the Making of *House of Incest*" (1987), Gunther Stuhlmann adds to and synthesizes the available information on the various catalysts, both inner and outer, of Nin's liberating prose poem. Making use of previously unavailable diary materials and letters, Stuhlmann addresses Nin's need to explore a style that would allow her to disguise diary entries as much as possible in order to make them publishable without offending anyone. He also offers that Nin derived the names "Alraune" and "Mandra" from a German film based on Hans Heinz Ewers's novel *Alraune*. The French title for the film was *La Mandragore*. Brigitte Helm, who starred in the film, also appeared in *L'Atlantide* (1932), "set in the fantastic underwater world of a sunken continent" (122). Stuhlmann presents these films, the statuesque Helms herself, perhaps even other roles Helms played, and the success of surrealism in film art as likely influences on *House*.

How appropriate that the latest words about *House* should be about its becoming, which is so much the burden of the book itself.

Winter of Artifice

First published as *The Winter of Artifice* by the Obelisk Press (Paris, 1939), this collection of two or three of Nin's longer stories (depending upon edition) is more commonly known by the title of later editions in which the article is dropped. In its earliest form, it contained "Djuna," "Lilith," and "The Voice." Beginning with the Gemor Press edition (New York, 1942), the "Djuna" story (a thinly disguised rendering of Nin's relationship with Henry Miller and his wife June) is suppressed.[2] What was "Lilith" is now untitled, and "The Voice" keeps its title. Both of the remaining stories have been rewritten. As included in the Dutton edition of *Under a Glass Bell and Other Stories* (New York, 1948), the stories – now "Djuna" (the story originally called "Lilith") and "The Voice" appear as part 1 and part 2 of "Winter of Artifice." (Thus, reviews of this edition contain comments on *Winter*.) Finally, in the Swallow edition (Denver, 1961), there are "three novelettes": "Stella" (a new addition of material removed from a novel), "Winter of Artifice" (the final title for the "Lilith" to untitled to "Djuna" item), and once again "The Voice."[3]

It is useful to keep in mind the various configurations and changing titles in order to know which items the criticism from different periods is addressing. For convenience here, the story with the changing title (involving a woman's relationship with her father) will be referred to by its final title, "Winter of Artifice" (or "Winter").

According to Nin, the Paris *Winter* came into print just as she was relocating to New York. There was little chance, in this upheaval, to get out review copies and establish distribution channels. This book, like her previous one, was part of a series of titles (this time called the Villa Seurat Series) by Nin and her friends. Now, Lawrence Durrell was the third member of the triumvirate along with Nin and Miller. It is not surprising, then, that one of the earliest reviews is by another member of the circle, Alfred Perlès, who praises Nin's style but seems artfully awestruck and befuddled about how to handle her subject matter and vision. Perlès favors the "Lilith" section, noting her ruthless inversion of the father theme and asserting that "Nin's art borders on a weird variety of clairvoyance" (47). He gives less attention to "The Voice" and none at all to the opening story. An interesting, detailed review by Emily Hahn notes a growth in Nin's art and vision through the three stories. Hahn finds the first (the one later suppressed) "immature and romantic," the second far more sophisticated in insight, and the third even more worldly-wise in its main character's recognition of "where it is wise to stop hoping" (437).

The Gemor Press edition brought forth a small flurry of comment, much of which emphasizes the fact that Nin's fictions are extensions or elaborations of her diaries. This interest deflects attention from the works themselves, whether the critic's judgment is negative or positive. In the *Herald Tribune* book section, Elaine S. Gottlieb considers the book "merely a continuation of the diary" and finds its two parts less satisfactory examples of Nin's art than two much shorter stories that had appeared in the periodical *Twice a Year* ("Birth" and "Woman in the Myth"). Gottlieb argues that "Winter" is a good story "that loses itself in the telling" and that "The Voice" suffers from the disconnectedness of some of its parts. In *The Nation*, Paul Rosenfeld, a critic with whom Nin had become friendly, admires the person behind the veiled autobiography, but says little about Nin's accomplishment as a writer of fiction.

The first extended treatment of *Winter* is by William Carlos Williams. In " 'Men . . . Have No Tenderness': Anaïs Nin's 'Winter of Artifice' " (1942), Williams struggles to articulate his approval of Nin's search for a female approach to writing. He senses that "a titanic struggle is taking place below the surface not to succumb to . . . that maelstrom of hidden embitterment which engulfs so many other women as writers" (430). He has some shrewd remarks to make about the relationships between the two stories, the outcome of the first allowing for the kind of development of character that takes place in the second. For Williams, Nin is on the verge of escaping from the stereotypical female style that is either man-defined or reactionary: she takes "a positive attitude toward her opportunities" (433). Yet it is clear that he finds her work fully successful only in isolated passages; his praise is more for her courage and potential than for what she has realized in this book.

Though Williams offers qualified praise, Nin's first reaction was to feel damned by it. She thought that both Rosenfeld and Williams had misread her by approaching her writing too much as autobiography (*Diary* 3: 204-5). But Williams is one of the first major literary voices to insist that Nin was to be taken seriously, that she was – or could be – more than a coterie writer. He also points to passages that he admires and clearly addresses them *as writing*. In Nin's complaint that Williams invented "an antagonism between men and women which I never considered," Nin seriously misreads her own work; and in her dismay over his caution, she misses the positive elements in Williams's remarks.

In his chapter on this title, Oliver Evans begins by misstating its confusing publication history (ignoring the fact that there were three stories in the Paris edition, claiming that the first part was called "Winter of Artifice" when in fact no part of that publication was so named, and missing the Gemor Press version altogether).[4] By treating "Stella" in his discussion of *Ladders to Fire* (of which it was originally a part), Evans causes some unnecessary confusion for those most familiar with the only readily available – Swallow – edition of *Winter*.

Having decided to address the work as it appears in the Dutton edition of *Under A Glass Bell and Other Stories*, Evans can rightly claim that "the title *Winter of Artifice* as applied to both stories is rather misleading, since it has reference only to the romance between the girl and her father" (44). But since Nin herself showed awareness of this in both earlier and later editions, it seems that the usually enthusiastic critic has here gone out of his way to register a complaint. Furthermore, he does not clarify the real crux of the problem in the Dutton edition – that Nin had formally identified "Djuna" and "The Voice" as part 1 and part 2 of *Winter*, not more loosely as related titles under an umbrella.

Appropriately, Evans gives most of his attention to the "Djuna" story, first warning readers against reading it (or "The Voice") autobiographically. Observing that the text is ambiguous regarding the physical nature of the father-daughter relationship, Evans insists that physical love in any case has nothing to do with the story's "stern underlying moral: that it is fatal for the lover to invent an a priori image of the beloved, since the strain of living up to this image destroys the ease and naturalness of the relationship" (46-47). The incestuous configuration, Evans argues, is symbolic in the same way that the title *House of Incest* is symbolic.

To his credit, Evans notes the close resemblance between the "Djuna" story and *House*, but he does not follow up with the biographical and bibliographical evidence. (At one time Nin had a work in progress that included materials later divided between *House* and "Winter.")

The narrative thread of "Winter" is straightforward and the narration is self-glossing, thus there is little here for Evans (or anyone else) to interpret. Evans does a workmanlike job of summarizing the story line and underscoring the key dramatic moments. He also pays careful attention to the symbolic gestures and image-motifs that Nin employs, wondering, for instance, if the obsessive hand-washing used to characterize the father is too much of a cliché. Additionally, Evans argues that the story reveals "a sly, sophisticated, and intensely feminine" sense of humor (55). He notes, also, the general resemblance to Lawrence's style of characterization and the specific echo of Poe's Roderick Usher.

Evans calls "The Voice" Nin's weakest longer narrative, observing that Lilith and Djuna are not sufficiently distinguished from one another. He surmises that while alternate separation and fusion of the characters may be deliberate, the effect, in certain places, is bound to confuse the reader – and may reveal a confused author (59). In contrast, he applauds Nin's handling of the relationship between Lilith and the Voice (the analyst), and he praises the italicized dream passage with which the story ends. In this passage and elsewhere in the story, Evans discovers Nin's characteristic – eventually obsessional – use of water images that reveal psychological states.

Evans examines "Stella" as part of *Ladders to Fire*, from which Nin eventually removed it. He provides a sure-handed summary of the plot, noting its tenuous connection to *Ladders* and its relationship to "Winter." He calls it the most Lawrentian of Nin's narratives and also one of her best, applauding how she has energized "the timeworn theme of the possessive female" (98).

In *The Mirror and the Garden: Realism and Reality in the Writings of Anaïs Nin* (1971; 1973), Evelyn J. Hinz develops a thesis concerning three controlling ideas – Karma, Tropism, and Fixation – in Nin's novels. She chooses to demonstrate how these themes develop through a series of novels by examining the progress of Djuna, treating her appearance in "Winter" as "a variation of the fixation motif" (43). The state of fixation, caused by her father's desertion, is manifest in such behavior as withdrawal and artificial role-playing. Karmic punishments torture both father and daughter, leading Djuna to an awareness that helps her throw off her fixation.

In "The Voice," Hinz finds Djuna at a later stage of her development. Now Djuna needs "to find a way of accepting the flow of life and the eternal metamorphosis that is characteristic of it without becoming submerged and stripped of her identity by it" (44). While Djuna reaches new levels of awareness and possibility through her interviews with the Voice and in her relationship with Lilith, the movement toward resolution of her conflict is detailed in a later work, *The Four-Chambered Heart*.

In *Collage of Dreams* (1977; 1981), Sharon Spencer notes that "Winter" is Nin's first mature adaptation of musical structures to her prose, addressing also the associated metaphor of dance (26-27).

More significant is her discussion of "The Voice," one of the few Nin titles that Spencer takes time to examine in some detail. She finds this story to be a remarkably effective illustration of how Nin uses dream and dream qualities in her art. The "seemingly random selections of characters and incidents" (58) have the logic of dream, and the flowing motion identified with dream work is manifest in Nin's "contrasting rhythms of rising and falling" (60). Balanced against the images of ascent and descent are those of horizontal motion through which the characters ready for transcending neurosis move out of themselves and mix with others in communal life (61).

Bettina L. Knapp calls the original two stories of *Winter* "antinovelettes" that defy the conventions of plot and characterization. After summarizing each briefly, Knapp provides a detailed analysis of Nin's attempt to fuse dream, reverie, and stream-of-consciousness technique. On this latter feature, Knapp compares Nin's work to Virginia Woolf's. Knapp examines how "Nin gives the reader the impression of experiencing two worlds concomitantly: linear time in the conscious frame of reference and the cyclical time scheme as the unconscious pursues its lucid course" (73). Knapp also points out the influence of Proust, particularly with regard to Nin's handling of time.

Detailed explorations of each novelette follow in which Knapp unravels the suggestions radiated by key images. These discussions are effectively presented to underscore stylistic and thematic points, but Knapp's more important work is found in her preliminary observations about techniques and affinities. (Note: Like Evans, Knapp treats "Stella" when discussing *Ladders to Fire*, where Stella is seen as someone not yet past the father-daughter crisis handled in "Winter" and "The Voice," 99-101.)

Franklin and Schneider are the first to present and make use of the publication history of *Winter*; they are also the first to base their interpretative discussion on the 1961 (Swallow edition), thus they attend to "Stella" as part of Nin's final plan for this book whereas earlier critics either ignore it or treat it separately from the titles with which Nin eventually associated it.

After a rehearsal of the structure and themes of "Stella," Franklin and Schneider examine its placement as the first of the three novelettes in the final *Winter*. They observe that because it is partly concerned with a father-daughter relationship, it provides an effective introduction to "Winter" in which that relationship is fully elaborated. Their reading of "Winter" is based on this association – so much so, in fact, that they address the unnamed daughter as "Stella" rather than as "Lilith" or "Djuna" as the earlier configurations of *Winter* would suggest. Thus, Stella's failed relationships with Bruno and Philip (in "Stella") find elucidation in the father-daughter problem of "Winter."

Another important contribution that Franklin and Schneider make is to stress the rare elaboration Nin gives to a male character in "Winter." They find Nin's full-dress portrait of "a man of the mind and not of the heart" reminiscent of Hawthorne's Chillingworth, Aylmer, and Ethan Brand (29). Notwithstanding their setting forth of original contexts and points of emphasis, the interpretive discussion of "Winter" brings no major new insights. Indeed, one begins to suspect that much of Nin's art is only too accessible thematically – that everything is available at first glance. Still, none do a better job of clearly reviewing the main incidents, methods, and consequent understandings than Franklin and Schneider.

Their treatment of "The Voice" is also admirably lucid and straightforward. They offer reasons for this title being placed last in the various *Winter* editions: the shift from a focus on one or two chief characters to the dispersed focus on many, and the new interest in the healer as well as those seeking help. Franklin and Schneider find that "the four patients are fairly well drawn and fully presented" (34) as they extract the central dilemma of each. They accuse Nin of teasing readers with the modern, ironic tragedy of a desperately troubled healer, but not following through. To conclude their discussion, Franklin and Schneider observe that the three-story *Winter of Artifice* presents women seeking self-understanding and wholeness "after having had their emotional and psychological growth stunted early in life. This is the subject of *House of Incest*, and it was to remain Nin's primary concern throughout all of her other works" (39).

Scholar's brief attention to *Winter* is surprising, even granting her relatively low estimate of Nin's fiction. Like Franklin and Schneider, she treats the Swallow edition, seeing this collection as "three variations on the double theme" first introduced in *Winter* (90). Scholar believes that this repetition becomes tedious and unproductive, in part because Nin reveals herself an unremarkable stylist.

Of the three pieces, Scholar ranks "Stella" highest because most emotionally intense and poetically concentrated. Scholar, characteristically, works back and forth between the story and the source diary materials, pointing out how the actress's unreconciled private and screen selves reflect not just Nin's observations about Louise Rainer, which she can objectify somewhat and gain artistic control over, but also Nin's own predicament of public and private selves, over which her artistry flounders.

Scholar is highly critical of "Winter," which she views as a failed "attempt to dramatize one of the major legends of her life-work: her reunion with her father" (93). Moreover, Scholar feels that Nin's mixed styles and partial revelations are not so much productively artful as they are self-protective in an unattractive way. For Scholar, lessons about the destructiveness of mask-wearing are not convincingly learned by the female character or her creator in this "flawed novella which substitutes indirection and innuendo for a full rendering of the father-daughter story" (96).

Scholar finds "The Voice" only slightly more successful but at least interesting as an experiment. The characters in this piece (based on Nin's relationship with Otto Rank) are difficult to distinguish from one another, and the Voice remains a symbol in this story in which nothing is sufficiently developed.

My own discussion of this story, and related *Diary* passages, demonstrates the ways in which many of Nin's early fictions are forthcoming on personal matters for which the published diaries are (or were) reticent. "The Voice" supplements the diary passages on the Rank-Nin relationship, suggesting that Rank was a failed suitor as well as analyst, employer, and mentor. Lilith and Djuna, as they articulate their feelings about the Voice, are finally two aspects of Nin wrestling with her feelings about a powerful yet vulnerable man who was becoming more and more demanding and possessive. Nin shows us Rank "playing out the old myth of the man creating the woman" (Jason 1986, 20) even though he was an articulate spokesman on the destructive consequences of this pattern.

"The Voice" and "Stella" are the exemplary works in Kazuko Sugisaki's "The Dream and the Stage: A Study of the Dream in Anaïs Nin's Fiction and in Japanese Noh Drama" (1986). Sugisaki maintains that the process of distillation by which Noh drama represents emotional truth and the possibilities of an individual's multiple identities is quite similar to the process revealed in Nin's renditions of dreams. In the two stories, the dream exists as a stage "where only the essence of reality, of truth, is concentrated" (97).

Under a Glass Bell

With her own Gemor Press publication of her short story collection, *Under a Glass Bell*, Nin's critical fortunes changed for the better, if only briefly. Finally, a critical giant waxed enthusiastic in a prominent setting. Edmund Wilson's *New Yorker* review of April 1, 1944 tells the world that although Nin's early books had been "a little disappointing," she has now published something that gave "a better impression of her talent." Wilson compares Nin's work to that of Virginia Woolf and to the surrealists, finding it superior to the latter: "Miss Nin is a very good artist, as perhaps none of the literary Surrealists is." He singles out "The Mouse," "Under a Glass Bell," "Rag Time" (spelled "Ragtime" in later editions), and "Birth" for special praise, and he ends by telling readers that the book was "well worth sending for." Wilson's enthusiasm along with promising words about Nin's longer fiction from Gore Vidal led to Nin's first affiliation with a major press, E. P. Dutton, beginning in 1946.[5]

Wilson's praise was not without qualification, and the other major review of this edition, by Isaac Rosenfeld in *The New Republic*, judges the book disappointing – not at all the forward step for feminine writing that the reviewer had been led to expect. Rosenfeld senses in Nin a writer whose stories do not have their own life, but rather shadow her own. He does praise the small-scope delicacy of her writing and the craftsmanship and design of the best stories. However, in Rosenfeld's view the hand of artifice prevails over any compelling feminine instinct.

The 1948 Dutton edition of *Under a Glass Bell and Other Stories* (which includes the two-part "Winter of Artifice") received much more attention than the privately printed Gemor title, but the reviews were often negative. In a pre-publication review, *The Virginia Kirkus Service* is decidedly and characteristically unsympathetic. Robert E. Kingery, writing for *Library Journal*, offers some faint praise for the feminine vision of the stories. A reviewer for the *Herald Tribune Weekly Book Review* and Robert Gorham Davis in the *New York Times Book Review* stress Nin's mixture of fact and fantasy and the obsessive, self-absorbed nature of both the author and her characters. In her *Partisan Review* "Fiction Chronicle" Elizabeth Hardwick finds some of the stories effective but the book as a whole tediously abstract with "too much straining for the exotic and a pathological appetite for mystification" (707). Vincent Garoffolo in the *New Mexico Quarterly Review* writes that Nin's materials are "genuinely fresh and important" but that she produces "vapid and monotonously uncertain" strivings, "laborious displays of insight into terribly fathomable matters" (248-49). In his *Hudson Review* comments, Vernon Young recognizes stretches of brilliance in Nin's style and asserts that "when Anaïs Nin is writing on her master subject, the interior stresses of the female personality, she has no equal" (427). Though he singles out "Hejda" for praise, Young questions the obsessively repeated theme of women who define men primarily as enemies. Indeed, he senses a "Sapphic odor" in Nin's writing. While appreciating her delineation of the fragmentation of modern city life, Young also faults Nin's uncertain handling of unconventional techniques and structures.

This volume was Nin's third with Dutton following the appearance of her first two novels, and the unfavorable reviews along with slow sales may account for it being her last. After 1948, references to this collection are infrequent until the British edition published by Peter Owen twenty years later.[6] In that same year, Oliver Evans's chapter "Houseboats, Veils, and Labyrinths: *Under a Glass Bell*," initiates the serious academic discussion of Nin's short stories.

Evans considers *Under a Glass Bell* to be "one of Nin's best books and one of the most distinguished short story collections published in this country in the forties" (64).[7] He compares it to Joyce's *Dubliners* both in style and in how it anticipates later work. Distributing the stories into three categories, after providing a synopsis of each story, Evans shows their thematic interrelationships as well as their connections to Nin's earlier work. The fantasies include "Houseboat," "Ragtime," "The Labyrinth," and "Through the Streets of My Own Labyrinth." The second category, "realist sketches," embraces "The Mouse," "Birth," and "The Child Born Out of the Fog." Evans considers the first two of these among Nin's masterpieces. To the third category belong those pieces that are essentially character sketches, most of which are based on actual people. "Hejda" (which Evans treats at some length and defends against Trilling's charges [see p. 55]), "Under a Glass Bell," "The Mohican," "Je Suis le Plus Malade des Surrealistes," "The Eye's Journey," and "The All Seeing" comprise the last group.

Evans perceives an advance of Nin's art in this collection. Her work now is less obscure and less dependent upon autobiography and biography. Her symbolism is now under greater control and in more effective balance with realistic elements. There is a hint of whimsical humor to relieve the uniform solemnity of her earlier work. He considers the title story to be perhaps Nin's finest stylistic achievement, while "Hejda" he finds a highly sophisticated performance whose depiction of the interaction of conscious and unconscious forces at work on the individual psyche anticipates the manner of Nin's novels.

Perhaps picking up the hint from Evans's references to likenesses between Poe's Roderick Usher and certain hypersensitive characters in Nin's early fiction, John Tytell develops an extended comparison between Poe's story and "Under a Glass Bell." In "Anaïs Nin and 'The Fall of the House of Usher' " (1973), he traces a literary legacy from Poe to the symbolists to Nin, noting the similarity between Nin's mixing of dream and consciousness and Poe's awareness of phantasmagoria. Though he finds some resemblances in setting and mood, Tytell stresses the similarities between Roderick Usher and Jeanne. Both are hypersensitive, both "are extremely responsive to the sentience of the environment" (7), both are unable to free themselves from the suffering of others, both are associated with the guitar, both end up in a "self-induced purgatory" (10). For Tytell, these numerous correspondences suggest that Nin is writing her own modern version of Poe's story.

Another essay on an individual story is Fred Watson's brief "Allegories in 'Ragtime': Balance, Growth, Disintegration" (1976). Watson discerns the central theme as "the balance of control between the conscious mind, symbolized by the narrator, and the subconscious mind, symbolized by the ragpicker" (1). He also discusses the story's perplexing, obscure conclusion.

In his "The Importance of *Under a Glass Bell*" (1977), Kent Ekberg argues that the collection can be approached as a novel. The stories, he observes, gain "unity and force through accretion" (7) as well as through repeated patterns of "reciprocity and doubleness" (14). Ekberg's comparisons are to *Dubliners, Winesburg, Ohio*, and *In Our Time*. He finds it useful to group the stories by theme and situations, perceives "Ragtime" to be the central story thematically, and announces Nin's major theme as "self-realization through spontaneous expression of emotions in relationships with other human beings" (8). Ekberg considers *Bell* a turning point in which Nin for the first time achieves an appropriate balance between subconscious and conscious vantage points and between closed and open forms.

Another discussion of the collection as a whole, and one of the more patient analyses of Nin's writing, is Keith Cushman's "The View from *Under a Glass Bell*" (1978). After pointing to the fifteen year evolution of the collection's final design, he compares *Bell* to Sherwood Anderson's *Winesburg, Ohio* and William Faulkner's *Go Down, Moses*, "all volumes in which the individual stories combine and cohere to form a unified fiction" (110). Cushman faults Evans's presentation of story groupings, arguing that "such categorization rends asunder what is really joined" (110). Without dismissing the variety, Cushman insists that there is a single vision, a single narrative stance, and a unifying orchestration of images, motifs, and language.

For Cushman, the main unifying image is that of the title story. The glass bell encloses and imprisons. He connects it to the images of entrapment that run through the other stories. With a poet's sense of form, Nin has built a structure of images that allows the various pieces to echo and amplify one another. Cushman's careful presentation of evidence demonstrates how Nin has built a whole larger than the sum of its parts.

Cushman not only speaks of the book's design in terms of unifying images and motifs, he observes the rationale behind the positioning of the stories. "Houseboat" leads off because it establishes the central themes. "Ragtime" is centrally located because it articulates both the very ways in which the stories are unified and the theme of transmutation. "Birth," the final story (examined at length), collapses and summarizes the still uncompleted movement from fantasy to reality that is the book's essential movement, though one that is consciously frustrated by Nin's wish to demonstrate that fantasy and reality are ultimately inseparable. Aside from examining these strategic placements, Cushman asserts that Nin has built *Bell* "on a series of pairings" (117) that create a sub-architecture of lesser consequence than the overriding poetic unity.

The history of Nin's opening story, "Houseboat," receives careful scrutiny by Benjamin Franklin V in his "The Textual Evolution of the First Section of 'Houseboat' " (1978). Franklin's concern is to demonstrate that Nin was a "diligent craftsman" who was not easily pleased with her work and made frequent revisions. He traces the development of "Houseboat" from an earlier published sketch called "Life on the Seine" (1941). Though the changes are both stylistic and substantive, Franklin stresses the latter. He reviews the two Gemor editions (both 1944), the Dutton (1948), and a version that appeared in *MD Medical Newsmagazine* (1971). Franklin argues that Nin's maturation as an artist and her quest for perfection led her to improve upon work even after it had appeared in print. However, she was "an imperfect examiner of her own work" (102) whose limitations hamper her status and restrict her audience, perhaps unfairly.

In their treatment of Nin's story collection in *Anaïs Nin: An Introduction* (1979), Franklin and Schneider agree with Evans that it is one of Nin's best efforts as a fiction writer. However, they rank it next to *House of Incest*, while Evans, as we have seen, finds it a more artistically mature work than Nin's earlier volumes. Franklin and Schneider are careful to distinguish between the original eight-story version (so highly praised by Wilson) which they admire, and the later (and standard) thirteen-story version of 1958 which they find diluted by significantly weaker material. Also, they introduce important issues of genre and evaluation by noting how dependent these stories are on *Diary* materials, some almost transcriptions from the *Diary*.[8]

In keeping with their distinction, the analysis that follows sorts out Nin's achievement in each story while underscoring her possible miscalculation in tampering with the high quality of the earlier version of the work. Franklin and Schneider give high marks to all of the early stories except for "The Mohican," which they feel is lacking in the dramatic tension and character relationships that make Nin's best stories successful. Those relationships are most often between a title character and the narrator. Another feature that Franklin and Schneider attend to is Nin's constant probing of the tension between the world of dream and that of reality. Here, they note her ambivalent relationship to the dream. While it may be a narcotic and a sanctuary, it is not where life can be completely lived. Nor is the aspect of nightmare absent. Returning frequently to this concern, Franklin and Schneider emphasize the thematic unity of the collection, paying less attention to the other unifying elements considered by Evans and Cushman.

Franklin and Schneider worry about Nin's tendency to stereotype, a habit signaled by a title like "The Mouse." On the other hand, they find in that very story an embryonic concern with social issues usually lacking in Nin's writing. They point out how the title story is a reworking of a section from *House of Incest*, and in this and other ways raise questions about Nin's powers of invention. For example, they do not hesitate to mention that the later addition, "Through the Streets of My Own Labyrinth," is not much more than a partial restatement of "The Labyrinth" which precedes it in the standard edition. Rather than defending "Hejda" as statement, as Evans and others do, they recognize and admit to its esthetically disturbing didacticism.

For all of their reservations, Franklin and Schneider still maintain that *Bell* reveals Nin near the top of her form. "Houseboat," "Under a Glass Bell," "Je Suis de Plus Malade des Surrealistes," "The Mouse," "Under a Glass Bell," "Ragtime," and "The Child Born Out of the Fog" are at least partial successes. "Birth," which concludes both the early and final editions, they judge to be "the most moving of Nin's stories" (59). By recognizing the unevenness and limitations of Nin's art, Franklin and Schneider create a context in which their qualified praise is often more meaningful than the unalloyed praise of other critics.

One of the odd features of Bettina L. Knapp's 1978 *Anaïs Nin* is the absence of material on this short story collection. The omission could not be accidental in a critical study that otherwise moves from title to title in Nin's career, and one is led to infer that Knapp finds this title of far less worth than Nin's other books. However, in " 'To Reach Out Further Mystically . . .' Anaïs Nin" (1979) Knapp exemplifies Nin's Lawrence-like intuitional reasoning through a discussion of the title story, "Under a Glass Bell." The analysis is preceded by an overview of Nin's interest in alchemical processes and symbols – an interest Knapp discusses in her book as well. (Indeed, the essay reads like a recycling of material Knapp may have originally intended to include in her book.)

Knapp relates the shape of the bell to "Pythagorean cosmogony" while finding it an androgynous image that links male and female forces (80-81). The glass material is remarkable for its transparency; in the story, it is "a way to the soul; the point from which a central system of coordinates radiates, setting the stage for feelings of sadness, tears, and pain to prevail" (81). Knapp emphasizes the nonrepresentational nature of the world signaled by the bell, the glass, and the enclosed house. The key images create not an inner experience but "an inner correspondence" (83), a way to make "the indeterminate palpable" (84). Though Knapp's treatment parallels her handling of Nin's other works in *Anaïs Nin*, it seems less accessible removed from the larger context. Throughout the essay, the title is italicized, suggesting that the entire collection is under scrutiny, but in fact Knapp only treats the title story.

Nancy Scholar shares the view that *Under a Glass Bell* includes some of Nin's best writing. She comments, "The condensed format of the short story was perfectly tailored to Nin's gifts and limitations as a writer" (98). These limitations include problems with structure on the large scale demanded by novels. For Scholar, *Under a Glass Bell*, like almost all of Nin's fictions, is best thought of as "a companion piece to the Diary" (99). By emphasizing this connection, Scholar means to underscore not only the centrality of the *Diary* to Nin's overall achievement, but the way in which knowledge of the *Diary* adds depth and context to writings that otherwise often seem fragmented, incomplete, and obscure. These characteristics suggest that Nin may have calculated her fictions as lures to bring readers to the diary. On the other hand, so filled with the diary herself, Nin may have simply miscalculated what readers would need, unable to avoid granting them some impossible intimacy with the unpublished work.

The stories Scholar singles out for special attention are "Birth," "Houseboat," "The Labyrinth," and "Hejda." In her treatment of each, she characterizes the relationship between the finished story and the *Diary* source. In the case of "Birth," Scholar finds the *Diary* version fuller and more satisfying. More importantly, Scholar shows how the two versions, while overlapping considerably, have significantly different thematic emphases. While both raise tension from the conflict depicted in the woman between holding on and letting go, only the story version crystallizes the theme of "a woman's struggle to give birth to her own identity" without the sanction or aid of man (101).

"Houseboat" takes *Diary* material and reforms it through abstraction and poeticizing. Nin focuses the legend of self that the *Diary* undertakes by distancing the narrator from those ordinary others who live their time-locked lives on land. The narrator is free from their pain, but nevertheless locked in her dreamworld. The final movement involves both loss and possible gain. Forced to abandon the houseboat, the narrator may be ready for a larger life. Scholar's almost affectionate examination of this story is somewhat undercut by her final reference to it as a "charming piece [that] provides a light accompaniment to the description of 'La Belle Aurore' in Diary II" (103).

For those who are familiar with the *Diary*, "The Labyrinth" will have a special haunting power unavailable to those who do not know first hand Nin's major work and her mixed attitudes toward it. Scholar finds a genuine passion in Nin's meditation on her relationship to the *Diary* and in her development of the labyrinth metaphor. Though she does not say so directly, Scholar implies that Nin is convincingly and uncharacteristically honest here in revealing both the lure and costs of autobiographical writing.

Scholar praises "Hejda" as the best of Nin's character sketches, having "a range and perspective" rare in Nin's work (105). Although Scholar considers Nin once again guilty of overexplaining, she also finds a refreshing (and unusual) touch of irony in the narration. Scholar reviews the plot, making her usual pertinent references to *Diary* sources, and concludes by considering the ironic regression that points to danger in the sought unveiling of the genuine woman disguised by man's designs: "growth has destructive potentialities for the modern woman" (106).

Touching upon a number of the other stories briefly, Scholar notes the comprehensive arch of the title story's metaphor. She also insists, though Nin and some of her critics believe otherwise, that none of the stories, certainly not "Ragtime" or "The Mouse," give us characters who fully escape the confines of the glass bell.

The "Erotica" and Other Early Stories

Shortly before her death, Nin agreed to the publication of a number of erotic short stories that she had written early in her career. *Delta of Venus* (1977) and *Little Birds* (1979) add little to Nin's stature, even though they sold amazingly well. Much of this work was composed "to order" during the early 1940s for – Nin then believed – a private collector. Perhaps because of this circumstance, Nin seems to have been able to keep an audience in mind in ways that often escape her in the main body of her work.

In the revised edition of *Collage of Dreams* (1981), Sharon Spencer includes a chapter on the erotica in which she remarks on the sheer variety of erotic doings as well as the "spirit of innocence" that characterizes these tales. Furthermore, Spencer observes that the standard narrative manner of the erotic tales reveals Nin's competence at straightforward story telling and thus persuades us that the idiosyncrasy of style in Nin's major works is the consequence of a calculated effort at something unique. Spencer judges *Delta* the superior collection, though both share the theme of praise for the human body in all its variety and "both suggest that sex is a desirable activity in and of itself" (122). In the context of Nin's total *oeuvre*, these collections underscore the centrality of the principle of Eros in all of her writing.[9]

In her playful, brainy, and overcoded "Erotica: The Semey Side of Semiotics" (1981), Cathy Schwichtenberg tests the compatibility of semiotics and erotica by performing a semiotic assault on "Lilith" from *Delta*. Schwichtenberg explores the various significances of the book's title and then places Lilith, as story and character, into that network of significances. One can say no more about where her blend of send-up and sense takes us than to quote: "Ultimate closure and satiation is illusory and we must be referred back to the semiotic network" (36). Must we?

Daniel R. Barnes considers how the conventions of erotic writing restrict Nin's art as well as how she exploits traditional motifs in his "Nin and Traditional Erotica" (1982). That same year, Dennis R. Miller contributed *"Delta of Venus*: Sex from Female Perspectives." Miller's method, which is to contrast passages from Nin's erotic tales with passages from Henry Miller's *Tropic of Cancer* and *Tropic of Capricorn*, shows how Nin consciously and successfully answers the challenge of maintaining a woman's voice and vision in a male genre.

More substantial than the earlier treatments is Smaro Kamboureli's "Discourse and Intercourse, Design and Desire in the Erotica of Anaïs Nin" (1984). Kamboureli examines Nin's own distinction between erotica and pornography, arguing that *Delta* and *Little Birds* fall closer to the pornographic. Yet these stories are pornography with a difference, thus Nin's deliberate labeling of them as "erotica." Kamboureli finds Nin "innovative within the realm of pornography" (144). While her focus is almost exclusively on her characters' sexual lives, other biographical elements in these stories make them more than merely pornographic and invest them with the erotic motif of desire. Moreover, the esthetic border around Nin's pornographic scenes enhances the dimension of desire that is the hallmark of the erotic. Finally, Nin's poetic sensibility and language transform her material.

In his "The Making of *Delta of Venus*" (1986), John Ferrone, Nin's editor at Harcourt Brace Jovanovich, tells the story of Nin's early reluctance and eventual capitulation regarding the publication of the erotica. Ferrone characterizes the manuscripts, which he was given a free hand in editing, and he describes something of the editorial process. Ferrone argues that *Delta* offers "elegance of style and feminine sensibility applied to a literary form that was often gross, dehumanizing, and superficial" (42). Like Spencer, he considers Nin an important contributor to this marginal sub-genre.

Delta is center stage in Judith Roof's "The Erotic Travelogue: The Scopophilic Pleasure of Race vs. Gender" (1991). Roof finds that Nin's stories are metaphors for theater and brothel in their concern with spectacle and display. They also remind us of how pornography utilizes "multiple, exotic differences" (121) in a way that ultimately neutralizes those differences. Exotic difference accounts as well for the travelogue nature of Nin's book. Roof examines "The Hungarian Adventurer" in detail, characterizes the other tales briefly, and establishes connections with the writings of de Sade and with the film *Emmanuelle*.

Even less polished than the unrevised erotica are the previously unpublished stories culled from the Northwestern University manuscript collection and brought together as *Waste of Timelessness and Other Early Stories* (1977). These represent Nin's apprentice work and can only be of interest to those already fascinated by Nin's later efforts. The most carefully considered appraisal of this volume is Kent Ekberg's discussion (1977) in which he observes Nin's early interest in dream material and finds prototypes for the major female characters of her mature fiction. Valerie Harms, whose Magic Circle Press published this volume, describes these stories in her "Anaïs Nin, Witch of Words" (1975). Her article also provides flavorful information on early states of Nin's published work and on marginal notations by Henry Miller found among the manuscripts.

Notes to Chapter 4

[1]Evans's book is reviewed by Anna Balakian in *American Literature* and Melvin J. Friedman in *Contemporary Literature*.

[2]An excerpted version of this novella, titled "Hans and Johanna," appears in *Anaïs: An International Journal* 7 (1989): 3-22. See also my comment on the relationship between the original "Djuna" and *Henry and June* in "Dropping Another Veil" (31).

[3]An English volume that combines the Swallow versions of *Winter* and *House* (Peter Owen, 1974) precipitates British comment on these works.

[4]This and other knotty bibliographical problems in Nin studies are examined by Franklin in "Anaïs Nin: A Bibliographical Essay."

[5]The young Vidal, then working for Dutton, was one of a coterie of young writers drawn to Nin in these years. *Ladders to Fire* is dedicated to Vidal. Their friendship turned to hostility some time later.

[6]There was minimal attention to a British edition by Editions Poetry in 1947, to Nin's privately produced 1958 edition, or to the Swallow imprint of 1961. The 1968 Owen edition spurred comment by Kenneth Graham in *The Listener*, Malcolm Bradbury in the *Manchester Guardian*, and Barry Cole in *The Spectator*. Cole scorns the book; the others find it an appealing but limited achievement.

[7]But it is not the original collection of the forties that he examines. See Franklin (1974) for changing contents of this and other Nin titles.

[8]This troubled note is one consequence of Franklin and Schneider finishing their work with six *Diary* volumes in print. Evans, who makes a contrary claim, could only have examined the first two.

[9]Spencer's reference article on Nin in the *Critical Survey of Short Fiction* (1981) is a reliable guide to *Bell* as well as to the erotica and *Waste of Timelessness* stories.

5: Nin's Longer Fiction

NIN'S CAREER AS A NOVELIST spans approximately twenty years, beginning with the privately printed and structurally misshapen *This Hunger* (1945) and ending with an emblematic career coda, *Collages* (1964). Along the way, the five novels that make up Nin's "continuing" *Cities of the Interior* were published by a variety of publishers under a variety of conditions, inviting a wide range of commentary. Reviewed as separate works as they first appeared, the novels needed to be reassessed as segments of *Cities* when first collected (1959) and then again when the fifth novel in the sequence, originally titled *Solar Barque* (1958), was expanded, rechristened, and published separately as *Seduction of the Minotaur* (1961). The final authorial version of a one-volume *Cities* did not appear until 1974 when *Seduction of the Minotaur* replaced *Solar Barque*.

The *Cities of the Interior* Novels

Before she had articulated plans for a continuous novel, Nin published her last major Gemor Press title, a section of which would remain as part of the completed *Cities of the Interior*. Reactions to *This Hunger* (1945) were predictably mixed, a continuation of what James Korges has called the *New Yorker/New Republic* battle led respectively by Edmund Wilson and Isaac Rosenfeld. In his review, Wilson is a more reserved and cautious partisan than he was earlier, making the best of the fact that the purported novel's three sections do not connect. Rosenfeld, in a piece called "Psychology as Literature," finds Nin guilty of simplistic characterizations (categorizations, in fact), and he considers her vision of modern womanhood unconvincingly and unattractively narrow and negative.

Even more hostile is Diana Trilling, who blasts Nin's insufficiency as a psychoanalyst. Trilling finds "Hejda" particularly flawed. Nin's insights, she complains, "serve the sexual chauvinism and self-pity of the modern female writer of sensibility."

Nin soon recognized the structural inadequacies of *This Hunger* (made up of "Hejda," "Stella," and "Lillian and Djuna"), a book best understood as a sampler rather than as a novel. Her first step was to remove "Hejda" from it and relocate that story in the 1948 version of *Bell*. Nin's first Dutton title, *Ladders to Fire* (1946), was made up of the shrunken "This Hunger" (as part 1) to which Nin added "Bread and the Wafer" as part 2. By the time of the Swallow edition, the "Stella" section was removed and relocated as a segment of *Winter*. The remaining ("Lillian and Djuna") part of *This*

Hunger, simply called "This Hunger," and "Bread and the Wafer" are the only sections of the final version.

The early reviews of *Ladders* are almost entirely negative, though in a *New Yorker* piece Edmund Wilson notes that the post-*This Hunger* material is more effective than the earlier sections. While a few critics, like Kay Keith, are friendly toward Nin's effort, many others (Jex Martin, Jr., Herbert Lyons, and Harrison Smith) find this novel derivative, tedious, and petulant. In spite of this chorus of dispraise, Dutton hung on (or was pre-committed) for a second novel, *Children of the Albatross* (1947). With this publication, readers could begin to consider the larger design that Wilson's reviews of her last two publications and Nin's headnote promised. "The books," Nin wrote, "can . . . be read separately or can be considered as parts of a tapestry."

But *Children* was not a success with reviewers either. Robert Gorham Davis accepts Nin's work on its own terms, though his comments about her technique of abstraction and generality would hardly win her new readers. William Hart praises her prose style while worrying over obscurity of meaning. Richard McLaughin also praises Nin's style, but he observes that her characters lack concreteness and convincing individuality. One reviewer who writes enthusiastically about *Children* is Violet R. Lang. She discerns Nin's attention to inner reality and finds her remarkably adept at revealing "deep personal relationships by writing of them in those circumstances which interpret them, the moments of change, the moments of revelation, the time of terrible intensity" (163).

Reviewers of Nin's third novel, *The Four-Chambered Heart* (published by Duell, Sloan and Pearce early in 1950) continue to complain about the lack of action, the unattractively self-centered characters, and the constantly intrusive, editorializing narrator. All the ways in which Nin's fiction continues to ignore the conventions of social realism remain the targets of her attackers. However, this novel also attracts a significant degree of praise. Hayden Carruth considers it "some of the finest writing of our time," and René Fülop-Miller writes appreciatively of Nin's ability to transform psychological insight into a narrative of inner experience. Highly complimentary also are Charles Rolo's comments; Rolo praises the novel's "climate of . . . pure feeling" as well as Nin's ability to probe deeply into the problems that frustrate "the fusion of two human beings" and to celebrate "the importance and beauty of that fusion" (87).

However, Nin's career as a commercially viable novelist was not sustained by such comments. In order to bring the latter stages of *Cities of the Interior* to readers, Nin had to turn once again to self-publication. *A Spy in the House of Love* (1954), ostensibly published by the British Book Centre, was actually a private venture for which Nin established a distribution arrangement. In addition to another supportive review by Charles Rolo is Maxwell Geismar's sympathetic treatment called "Temperament vs. Conscience." Comments by Jerome Stone and Marvin Mudrick are respectively unenthusiastic and hostile. In an artfully sarcastic play of negatives, Mudrick writes: "It would be unfair to imply that Miss Nin is incapable of straightforward inanities" (614). In his adulatory "Notes pour une Préface" (1960), Jean Fanchette gives considerable attention to *Spy*, calling it Nin's best work.

Little notice accompanied what was temporarily the final installment of *Cities of the Interior*. *Solar Barque* (1958) was self-published (printed in Ann Arbor by Edwards Brothers) and then absorbed into *Cities* (1959), which in its first edition carried no publisher's imprint. In 1961, the same text of *Cities* was issued as from Alan Swallow who announced that this and other Nin titles were now added to his list. *Seduction of the Minotaur* received a separate Swallow publication that same year, misleadingly billed as a "brand new novel which sets the climax upon the Nin long fiction." Reviewers' attentions to the separately published *Seduction* and the collected *Cities* overlapped.

Seduction receives moderate praise from Patricia Hodgart, who applauds Nin's prose style and her insights into the exile theme while worrying that the novel is "littered with familiar surrealist images." An anonymous review ("Stuff of Dreams") in the *Times Literary Supplement* echoes Hodgart's enthusiasm for Nin's evocation of place but also, like Hodgart, finds the novel losing its essential focus and style in the later pages. Indeed, criticism of Nin's resolution through flashbacks is frequent in the reviews. Malcolm Bradbury, writing for *Punch*, finds the style and sensitivity insular and feminine. He praises the novel's intelligent insights but not its degree of self-consciousness. Adam Margoshes applauds Nin's evocation of the Mexican landscape and her skill at characterization. He also notes the contemporary nature of her concerns and their universality. Margoshes, like most critics familiar with Nin's earlier work, finds *Seduction* a step forward in its control over style.

The earliest comments on *Cities* seem more in the nature of promotion than criticism. Noteworthy for appearing a year ahead of the first edition of *Cities*, Edwin Fancher's "Anaïs Nin: Avant-Gardist with a Loyal Underground" (1958) is more interview than review. It rehearses the party line about Nin's importance as a prober into the feminine psyche. An unsigned piece by Nin partisan (and cousin by marriage) Kathleen Chase in *Two Cities: La Revue Bilingue de Paris* applies Nin's comments about D. H. Lawrence to an understanding of her own work. Chase discusses the symbolic nature of Nin's characterizations, the defensive internalization of their lives, and the ways in which they partake of their chosen environments.

Critics whose comments on *Cities* followed the 1961 Swallow commitment to bring all Nin's older work back into print while releasing her new titles already tended to view the continuous novel as the centerpiece of the complete *oeuvre* and to take the opportunity to comment on all of Nin's

Swallow titles. Most notable here are review-essays by Frank Baldanza, Oliver Evans, and Harriet Zinnes discussed in chapter two.

Review criticism and other kinds of commentary on the individual novels continued as Swallow brought out separate editions of the first four *Cities* novels and as editions (with some titles appearing even before the Swallow editions) became available for British and French readers. Worth noting here are Lawrence Durrell's friendly preface to the British edition of *Children* (Peter Owen, 1959) and James Korges's discussion of that same novel in his "Curiosities: Nin and Miller, Hemingway and Seager," published in 1965. Durrell provides only cursory, predicable old-friend praise ("her books are iridescent, held together by a finely-spun web of cross-references"), but Korges offers something quite different.

Korges is one of the first to mount a detailed attack on the praise accorded Nin by Miller, Wilson, and other enthusiasts. He briefly reviews Nin's critical reception ("that has misled a good many readers into thinking her a good novelist"), then goes on to attack the abstraction and sameness of her body of work. Having read Nin's pamphlet essays of the mid-forties, Korges suggests that Nin's theories, hopelessly confused in his view, lie behind the weaknesses in her art.

He then offers a lengthy discussion of *Heart*, which he believes is the best of her books. One of Korges's more interesting observations is that "Djuna is a remarkably stupid woman who only pretends herself wise," though he is certain that Nin means for readers to take Djuna seriously. He further contends that Nin seems to be striving toward an allegorical formula that does not quite work because her imagination (fortunately) outstrips the formulaic underpinning. The complex handling of character and motive in this work reaches a level Nin does not usually achieve. It is difficult to know whether Korges is damning the work with faint praise or praising the work with faint denigrations until the end when he writes: "I am not prepared to argue that this is a great novel; but it is a fine achievement by a minor, flawed novelist." Here Nin comes closest to achieving "a balance of intensity and control, of insight and art." Unfortunately, this "best of Nin's fictions is buried in the 700 pages of the repetitious, incoherently structured *Cities of the Interior*" (74).[1]

Not until Oliver Evans's *Anaïs Nin* (1968) are the interrelationships and individual merits of the five *Cities* novels addressed in a detailed and systematic way. Evans explores each novel at length, allotting a chapter to each. His balanced appraisal of *Ladders* begins with an overview of Nin's "general theory of fiction" and of her methods. In this overview, Evans pleads Nin's case against the critics who had disparaged her work (perhaps) out of ignorance of her intentions. The narrow range of characters in Nin's novels results, Evans argues, from the "enormously complicated" nature of her concern with discovering the true and genuine self underneath the many false selves humans project toward others. Nin's search for definitive motive and character (two inseparable concepts) would be bottomless unless she severely limited the number of characters that she explored. Thus, only a small handful of primary characters wind their way through the several novels, and other characters are defined only in relation to the central ones.

But Nin's thematic intentions are less original than her means. Since for Nin fiction *is* characterization, her techniques are all in the service of revealing character. Broadly, Nin's approach (as understood by Evans) is twofold: She presents readers "with the symbols encountered in the characters' dreams, daydreams, and fantasies" and she explores and interprets the identifying symbols "through the methods of psychoanalysis" (90). However, Nin's revelations of character, Evans states, do not depend on the narrator taking the psychoanalyst's role but rather "through a series of experiences leading to self-knowledge, or through the assistance of other characters" (90). Nin's art does not so much have story-telling as its end as it does "the direct revelation of experience" (91) through the employment of various poetic tools into her prose; notably, rhythm and repetition.

Evans is so much the sympathetic reader that he gets involved in near contradictions when he must recognize the extent of editorializing in Nin's work (which is indeed either through the narrator playing psychoanalyst or the unsubtle use of a particularly acute character to serve the same purpose). He is too much the trained critic not to recognize this problem or not to realize that Nin's admirable striving for the "essence" of character often leads to an excessive selectivity that leaves readers disoriented. Indeed, as he turns to his discussion of *Ladders*, Evans asserts that this early novel suffers from Nin's tendency to neglect most readers' needs for "variety as well as surface coherence" (93).

Taking as his text the Dutton edition, Evans gives considerable attention to "Stella," which he considers "one of this author's most thoroughly realized performances" (98), though it does not fit into the book's design. The "Lillian and Djuna" section he calls the most substantial and the most dramatically effective in presenting the core theme of "woman's search for completion" (98). Jay is rated as Nin's most fully realized male character, and the Jay-Lillian relationship "is the most successfully portrayed of the four which comprise the bulk of this section" (103). In his discussion of the second part of *Ladders*, "Bread and the Wafer," Evans points out the effective use of Faustin as a foil further to explore Jay's character and the late introduction of Sabina, a decision that is typical of the problems encountered in assessing Nin's novels "as independent organizations rather than as continuing units in a series" (106).

Evans cannot turn to advantage the observation he shares with earlier critics that Nin's female characters – Stella, Lillian, and Sabina – have overlapping traits that make it difficult to sort them out. The lack of surface context only complicates this problem, and the fact that they are intended as archetypes makes the possibility of confusion even more harmful: "if archetypes overlap they tend to lose their symbolic force" (112). Nevertheless, Evans insists that this admittedly flawed book contains "considerable beauty" and is "a worthy inaugurator of the series" (112).

While admitting to problems in *Children* as well, Evans finds Nin's second novel on the whole under firmer control. He reviews how in the first part, "The Sealed Room," Djuna is revealed through flashbacks and in her relationships with various young men. He pays particular attention to the theme of "distrust of the father figure" (118) as shared by Djuna and Paul, considered by Evans to be one of Nin's most successfully realized characters. In the second part of *Children*, "The Café," Evans finds a richer delineation of the three major female archetypes of *Cities* (Lillian, Sabina, and Djuna). The reader now knows them well enough to be concerned about them and to await the further complication of their lives.

With *Heart*, Evans believes that Nin created a work of greater unity than she had achieved hitherto. The restriction to three main characters, the relatively self-contained plotting, and the rounded exploration of theme (of the fallibility of human love) give it a life of its own distinct from its place in the *Cities* sequence. Yet he observes that it has stronger thematic ties to the sequence than does *Children*, which can be judged an interruption or digression. He notes, moreover, that the acclaim that it (*Heart*) has been accorded by other critics invariably depends on its closer correspondence "to the conventional idea of the 'well-made novel' " (141), and thus its success may be taken as another kind of denigration of Nin's characteristic manner. Through Evans's discussion of this novel, he makes useful comparisons to the work of Lawrence and, somewhat less expectedly, to that of Carson McCullers (the subject of his earlier book).

Evans finds links between the basic pattern of *Heart* and *Spy* as stories in which the protagonists reach new states of self-awareness (revealed in interior climaxes) after a series of frustrations. That is, Sabina's journey in the latter novel is like Djuna's in the earlier one. However, *Spy* is radically different from its predecessors, experimentally the most extreme. It forsakes chronology and causation altogether in favor of a "spatial" structure, and it mixes fantasy and reality in ways that challenge (if they do not frustrate) the unwary reader. Evans points out how Sabina's various relationships dramatize the warring fragmentation of self and praises Nin's success "at depicting the anxieties of self-division, the peculiar anguish and pathos attendant upon the attempt to lead a multiple existence" (150).

Though Evans notes that passages in *Spy* directly and without utility repeat passages from earlier novels (while other disturbing repetitions are internal), he prefers to stress what he considers the undeniable charm of this work. This charm he attributes to its stylization. Nin's poetic prose here provides passages of some of her best writing "of a kind that is relatively rare in English" (162).

For Evans, *Seduction* is notable in that the characteristic pattern of bringing a central female figure to awareness (this time it is Lillian) is carried a step further – to action. He also finds this novel the most complex in its use of symbolism and at least equal to *Heart* in its "concessions . . . to the tradition of the realistic novel" (163). Setting and character are related in a way unique among the *Cities* novels, and for the first time some of the characters are given surnames. Though lacking the unity of *Heart*, *Seduction* is more ambitious, more richly-textured, and more finished. Although many of the early reviewers objected to the final pages of this novel, in which Lillian's past is handled by flashbacks during her homeward trip to New York, Evans finds this an effective technique to reveal Lillian's new objectivity. He particularly praises the extended astronomical conceit with which this novel – and the continuous novel – ends.

Throughout his discussion, Evans provides detailed interpretive summaries of each work, pointing out stylistic and structural features and noting the points of contact among the five novels. His approach does not, however, allow a consideration of the whole.

As observed earlier, the two book-length studies that follow Evans's (Hinz's in 1971, Spencer's in 1977), while they tell us much about Nin's themes and techniques, do not proceed by exploring individual titles or the *Cities* composite (though Hinz provides a detailed treatment of Lillian as she appears in two of the novels and Spencer has made important contributions to assessing *Cities* in her other writings). We have to turn elsewhere to pick up the thread of how the *Cities* novels are treated by critics.

Perhaps the first detailed analysis of a Nin title to appear in periodical literature is Wayne McEvilly's "The Two Faces of Death in Anaïs Nin's *Seduction of the Minotaur*" (1969). McEvilly's Jungian approach considers archetypal patterns in Lillian's journey of self-discovery through analysis of the stages of that journey and of Nin's suggestive symbols. He approaches Nin's book as a wisdom text; the reader who is changed by it has truly understood it. Highly allusive, subjective, and enthusiastic, McEvilly nonetheless provides a compelling reading.

Duane Schneider's "The Art of Anaïs Nin" (1970) is concerned both with Nin's fiction and with the early *Diary* volumes, but draws its evidence about how Nin's writings achieve unity from an analysis of the first four *Cities* novels. Schneider isolates three methods: "1.) recurring characters, symbols, and motifs; 2.) direct and indirect psychological analysis; and 3.) the result of the first two: the definition of a single primary character" (507). After demonstrating how each of the four novels is centered in its primary character and how secondary characters are used, Schneider observes that the diary form allows Nin greater opportunity to exploit her methods of characterization. Thus, for Schneider, the *Diary* is the more successful artistic achievement.

Paul Griffith, in "The 'Jewels' of Anaïs Nin: *Cities of the Interior*" (1970), regrets the neglect of what he believes is Nin's major achievement. Organizing his discussion around the three major heroines, Griffith summarizes appreciatively while underscoring key themes, images, and techniques.

My own "Teaching *A Spy in the House of Love*" (1971) examines how the phases of Sabina's character are developed not only through her relationships with various lovers but also through accompanying allusions to a spectrum of composers, musical works, and styles of music. Also, "images of circularity" inform our understanding of Sabina's behavior and of the book's structure. That same year, a review ("Hothouse Crusader") of the English edition calls attention to Nin's "intriguing juxtaposition of fantasy with precise, accurately observed visual detail" and underscores the subtext of women's emancipation.

1974 brings a significant acceleration of Nin studies in general and attention to *Cities* in particular. The most important development is the first complete one-volume edition of the work with Nin's own preface and an introduction by Sharon Spencer. Also that year appears the first book-length collection of Nin criticism, Robert Zaller's *A Casebook on Anaïs Nin*, containing Spencer's "Anaïs Nin's 'Continuous Novel': *Cities of the Interior.*" Though Spencer's two essays overlap (the version in Zaller's collection is the earlier one), they are far from identical.

The *Casebook* essay is more elaborate. It likens the continuous structure of *Cities* to "the continuous, erratic, unpredictable process of personal growth" (68), thus making a rare case for naturalness in Nin's art. Spencer also likens Nin's structural method to the growth process of a large tree, to abstract expressionist painting, and to mobile and movable sculpture, developing useful insights from each comparison. Turning from structure to themes, Spencer underscores the radical content of Nin's novels, ranging from incestuous longing to homosexuality to an interracial affair. Finally, Spencer explores how the *Cities* novels dramatize the multiple dimensions of selfhood and the individual's need "to mediate among one's actual and potential selves in order to achieve the most expressive, the most fluid and mobile pattern of life possible to any individual" (75).

Spencer's introduction touches many of the same issues, but more briefly. It pays more attention than the *Casebook* essay to building a modernist context within which to place *Cities*, and it attends to the ideals of transformation and animation that appear everywhere in Nin's writing. As in the earlier essay, Spencer observes that the published order of the novels simply follows the order in which they where written. In fact, they can be read in any order because Nin's art and vision deny any "fixed starting point or concluding point" (xiii). Through analogies to the design of the Philosopher's Stone and through a brief discussion of how Nin uses the ancient theory of the four elements and their influence over personality, Spencer provides added insights into structure and imagery in *Cities*. For Spencer, *Cities* is a modernist masterpiece.

In yet another essay, *"Cities of the Interior*: Femininity and Freedom" (1976), Spencer examines how Lillian and Djuna variously succumb to and are at war with the conventional mothering role. She shows how Nin contrasts them with Sabina's "dramatic display of freedom" (12), while also acknowledging the price of that freedom. In this and other essays of the mid-1970s, Spencer is essentially building toward her comprehensive treatment of Nin's writing in her *Collage of Dreams*.

Also appearing in 1976 is Suzette Henke's "Anaïs Nin: Bread and Wafer," a Freudian reading of *Ladders* in which Sabina is said to represent the id, Lillian the ego, and Djuna the superego. Looking back and forth between the novel and its seed passages in *Diary* 1, Henke finds Nin transforming the psychodynamics of her life into literary understandings of herself and others.

Particularly intriguing and attractively written is Paul Brians's "Sexuality and the Opposite Sex: Variations on a Theme by Théophile Gautier and Anaïs Nin" (1977), one of the few comparative studies involving Nin's work. Brians demonstrates parallels between Gautier's *Mademoiselle de Maupin* (1836) and *A Spy in the House of Love*, especially in how each author explores "the nature and limits of sex roles by creating characters who take on certain emancipating characteristics of the opposite sex" (122). Brians explores the manner of each central character's role playing as well as what each learns from her adventures. He concludes with the observation that Gautier's story of Madeleine is merely "an entertaining fantasy" while Nin's (or Sabina's) story "is much more serious, much more authentic" (136). This is one of the few fully sympathetic discussions of *Spy*.

Somewhat less compelling is Anna Balakian's " '. . . and the pursuit of happiness': *The Scarlet Letter* and *A Spy in the House of Love*" (1978). Balakian argues that in examining the repercussions of adultery, Hawthorne and Nin "realize that they must view the social fomentation from the artist's position rather than the sociologist's, and it is in this respect that their objectives converge fundamentally" (163). Such an airy linkage suggests that the discussion must ultimately stress contrasts – and it does. Along the way, Balakian offers useful comments on Nin's quest for a healthier basis for human relationships and on Nin's distance from her protagonist.

In her 1978 *Anaïs Nin*, Bettina L. Knapp provides a fifty-three page chapter titled "A Renaissance Artist: *Cities of the Interior*." She offers a useful vision of *Cities* as a whole before examining its individual novel-units in five chapter subsections. Even more than Evans's treatment, then, Knapp's helps the reader attend to both the separate units and the overall design. Yet, within her discussions of each novel, Knapp makes very few connecting links. Nonetheless, her analyses are erudite and intelligent, marred only by a carelessness (here and throughout the book) about bibliographical facts.

For example, Knapp states that *Solar Barque* is part 1 of the fifth novel and that *Seduction of the Minotaur* is part 2 (95). This claim is utter nonsense. Knapp also states that the 1959 Swallow edition of *Ladders* is unpaginated (155), but there is no 1959 Swallow edition of *Ladders*. The first separate Swallow edition, 1966, is paginated, as was the first (Dutton) edition. The first edition of *Cities*, however, is unpaginated. Though a sympathetic and insightful reader of Nin's work, Knapp is probably the least reliable critic regarding its publication history.

In contrast to those critics who favor Nin's earlier and shorter fictions, Knapp points her book toward valuing *Cities* as Nin's major achievement. With *Cities*, Nin is "no longer the fledgling grasping and floundering about, she is now certain of her course, both literary and psychological, and of the techniques needed to achieve her goal" (95). Knapp develops her introduction to *Cities* through references to works by Balzac, Zola, and Nathalie Sarraute. In comparison with Sarraute, who has a similar interest in the intersecting zones of the conscious and unconscious, Nin's fiction world has far less abstraction: her characters "live in a very real and worldly environment" (98).

In discussing *Ladders*, Knapp chooses to treat the "Stella" section that had been removed by the time *Cities* was first brought together. She underscores the symbolic nature of Nin's characters and their actions, especially the way in which "Lilian's [sic] feelings of self-destruction and deprecation are conveyed" (106). Each character (Stella, Lillian, Djuna, and Sabina) is a magnification of some aspect of one or more of the others. Knapp is especially attentive to Nin's stylization of scene and setting in this work.

Knapp's analysis of *Children* addresses references and analogies to dance and to the spatial arts. Nin's characters seem to relate to one another ceremonially. Once again, Knapp is particularly useful in establishing the expressive values of Nin's settings as she contrasts the emotional atmospheres generated in the two parts of *Children*: "The Sealed Room" and "The Café."

Knapp calls *Heart* "the most poignant" section of the *Cities* sequence. Within her outline of the novel's events and tensions, Knapp offers that Zora might be the most interesting character, a convincing study of the hypochondriac. She and Rango "may be looked upon as facets of Djuna's personality, each in conflict with the other, each attempting to relate to the other" (127).

The shift in setting from Paris to New York with *Spy* brings with it a shift in emphasis and tone: "the youthful and romantic atmosphere of France" gives way to a discontent with America's puritanical culture. Knapp notes a concomitant shift in Nin's style, now closer to "the New Novelists' technique" in which there is "a further depersonalization of the main character" (131). *Spy* is explored in the context of polyphonic writing as Knapp draws parallels between Nin's work and that of Alain Robbe-Grillet, Michel

Butor, and Marguerite Duras. Knapp's familiarity with these and other Continental writers allows her to offer important perspectives on Nin's work otherwise rarely available (in English language criticism).

Though jumbled by her mishandling of titles and their contents, Knapp's discussion of *Seduction* maintains the high level of insight and energy characteristic of her ambitious study of the other *Cities* novels. "Sonorities, syntheses, inversions, antitheses, and repetitions are only a few of the literary devices used by Nin to set up an ever-widening pattern within the text, thus arousing infinite sympathetic vibrations in the protagonists as well as in the reader and, in so doing, expanding consciousness" (143). So Knapp characterizes *Seduction*, and, by implication, the winding experiment that it concludes.

Though she touches upon passages from various *Diary* volumes, the central text for Stephanie A. Demetrakopoulos's "Anaïs Nin and the Feminine Quest for Consciousness: The Quelling of the Devouring Mother and the Ascension of the Sophia" (1978) is *Heart*. Demetrakopoulos's general concern is with "the presence of the world mother and her personal mother in Anaïs Nin's psyche and literary works" (117). Jungian in orientation, this study fruitfully underscores the importance of "both the personal and transpersonal mother" in Nin's fitful pursuit of self-understanding and fulfillment. In *Heart*, Djuna (Nin's surrogate) kills off an aspect of herself that is self-destructive: "She cuts her mother out of her psyche" (126). This symbolic slaying of the mother (the "Devouring Mother") is a necessary act of liberation, an act paralleled in other literature and myth. Because of its clarity, focus, and richness of understanding, Demetrakopoulos considers *Heart* to be Nin's most enduring novel.

In their 1979 study, Franklin and Schneider pay close attention to the textual history of the *Cities* novels and to Nin's intentions as revealed in her introduction to the English edition of *Ladders* (1963). Though they consider the "continuous novel" among Nin's most ambitious experimental efforts, they consider its breadth of scope detrimental to her success.

Franklin and Schneider give *Ladders* the most detailed analysis found anywhere. They explore the intricate relationships among the major and minor characters, and they illustrate and assess Nin's use of nonchronological juxtapositions of narrative passages. More than other critics, they look closely at the male characters, Larry and especially Jay, whose behavior and motives are examined at length. They note, also, how although Lillian is the central character in this novel, the focus shifts to the more reflective and seemingly stable Djuna at the end.

The centrality of Djuna to *Children* and *Heart* (after her career as an important peripheral figure in Nin's earlier fiction and before her return to that status) provides the occasion for Franklin and Schneider to offer an astute analysis of the character who most resembles her creator. They perceive a woman who has sometimes seemed condescending, whose frequent role as confidante may not grow so much from her compassion for others as it does from her gifts at locating and unraveling the problems of others. Of course, now Djuna's own problems are explored. Because she is so much more rational than the other female characters, and because she is present-ed as having achieved an approximation of wholeness that they still seek, Franklin and Schneider observe that it is difficult for the reader to take Djuna's troubles to heart. Regarding matters of craft, Franklin and Schneider find the second part of *Children*, "The Café," to have a surface structure superior to anything of similar length that Nin had so far written.

They also observe that the first two units of the continuous novel may not be novels at all. Both *Ladders* and *Children* are "divided into two dis-tinct, titled, and relatively short parts" (99) that seem to stand on their own more than they relate to their companion parts. *Heart*, on the other hand, may be considered Nin's first full-fledged novel. However, rather than find in the greater unity of *Heart* a more successful work of art, as other critics have done, Franklin and Schneider find it weaker than the earlier long fic-tion. They attribute this relative weakness to two factors. First, the "grander scale" of a true novel is a scale Nin is not able to manage well; second, Nin here tries to develop a major male character, Rango, and fails to sustain the reader's interest in him. Aside from these striking judgments, the authors continue to provide detailed and reliable summary and interpretation. Their attention to bibliographical and textual matters is in evidence once again as they note a shift in emphasis caused by Nin's decision, with the Swallow edition, no longer to label the last forty-nine pages as "Part Two" but rather to provide a less emphatic break in the text.

Moving on to *Spy*, Franklin and Schneider consider it to be Nin's best-known novel because of the suggestive title and also because it has had more editions than any of her other works. However, aside from the shift to the New York setting, they find it substantially similar to her other titles. In treating this novel as a part of the *Cities* weave and as Sabina's turn for de-tailed probing, Franklin and Schneider do not make their usual evaluative distinctions but rather keep the discussion primarily descriptive. Most use-ful here are the comparisons to characters, situations, and techniques in Nin's other writings and to Sabina's appearances elsewhere. Unique to this discussion is a brief treatment of the short story called "Sabina," a piece of Nin's fiction left untouched by others.

Franklin and Schneider end their examination of the *Cities* series with a penetrating look at *Seduction*. They believe that the setting of Mexico, as Nin exploits it, "offers a perfect backdrop for the final development of Lil-lian from a troubled, unsettled woman into one who, at the end, is content in life with herself and her husband, Larry" (130). They explore the function of Lillian's characterization as a jazz musician, and they demonstrate how the novel's supporting cast is used to bring Lillian's journey toward self-knowledge to fruition. Finally, they assess the post-*Solar Barque* section of

Seduction, judging it an effective conclusion not only to the individual novel but to the entire *Cities* sequence. In concluding this chapter, the authors state: "Knowledge and acceptance of oneself is the key to Nin's perception of mature life, and that something so seemingly simple is in fact so difficult is the message of Nin's first five novels" (146).

Although they treat *Cities* and its sections with care and sympathy, Franklin and Schneider make no claims for Nin's achievement here. As noted earlier, they find Nin's first piece of fiction, *House of Incest*, to be her best and most original, and they feel that she is generally more effective as a fiction writer in shorter forms. They believe, as Nin herself came to, that the *Diary* is Nin's major achievement, and they suggest that Nin's nearly thirty-year attempt to win acceptance as a fiction writer was more or less misguided.

In his brief "Anaïs Nin's Allegories" (1979), Jon Rosenblatt insists that the "thoroughgoing allegorical structure" of *Cities* is connected to an older notion of time in which past and present are simultaneous. This concept of allegory is one way of explaining those nonchronogical junctures in the novels that cannot be treated as flashbacks. The allegorical concept, signaled by the tell-tale names of Nin's characters, also helps to justify the extensive use of repetition within the *Cities* sequence.

Sylvia Paine devotes a chapter to "Anaïs Nin" in her 1981 study, *Beckett, Nabokov, Nin: Motives and Modernism*. Paine's interest is in the way certain modernist writers "explore fully the role of the senses in advancing the process of self-transcendence" (7). In characterizing Nin's sacramental attitude toward sex, Paine draws most of her evidence from *Seduction* and a small amount from *Collages*. She finds *Seduction* the best illustration of Nin's vision because only Lillian among Nin's heroines attains a "unity of self and world" (79). Though Paine's treatment is detailed, it offers no advances. Moreover, Paine's attempt to find useful links among the three modernists she treats is not very convincing. The yoking context is flimsy, and the individual essays do not allow insights about one author to help readers understand the others.

Nancy Scholar's appraisal of the *Cities* sequence (1984) is the least generous of those made by the principal students of Nin's work. She believes that Nin's "intention is clearer than her achievement," allowing it "a fascinating work from the standpoint of Nin's cumulative self-portrait" but claiming that "from an aesthetic viewpoint it is problematic" (109). Scholar feels that Nin had developed habits in her diary-writing that did not serve her well either in developing a sense of audience or in establishing a distance on her materials that would make greater control possible. She finds the novels "formless, held together, like the Diary, only by the tenuous thread of the writer's projected personality" (110).

Scholar does not consider the separate novels that make up *Cities*. Instead, she divides her discussion into several thematic sections. In the one on "Woman's Struggle to Understand Her Own Nature," Scholar appreciates Nin's commitment to the struggle but finds her insights limited and contradictory. To the extent that Nin's success in portraying this struggle rests on her skills of characterization, Scholar finds even more to object to. Nin's "half-drawn" characters never materialize fully either in their suffering or in their movement toward completion. For Scholar, then, Nin's novels make no significant progress in revealing woman's nature.

In a passage called "Voyage without Compass," Scholar traces the leitmotif carried through the compass image of the quest for orientation and the fear of dispersion of identity. The disoriented feelings of Nin's protagonists, she suggests, are partly replicated by the situation in which Nin's problems with form leave the reader. In "Woman as Artist," Scholar finds it surprising–given Nin's concerns in the *Diary* and the fact that Lillian, Sabina, and Djuna are all artists–that *Cities* makes no exploration of either "the demands of their art or the conflicts of being a woman artist" (113). Only in Nin's presentation of Sabina as an actress does Scholar find an effective, convincing key to character. Lillian remains locked in female stereotypes while Djuna is both too idealized and too obviously the author's surrogate intelligence to take seriously.

In dealing with these and other matters, such as the problem of fragmentation and multiplicity, Scholar continues to charge Nin with failure to resolve anything in a convincing manner either formally or thematically. Where some critics find an attractive consistency in Nin's focus on process, Scholar finds a failure of vision, will, and craft. Considering in what low esteem Scholar holds much of Nin's work, it is sometimes difficult to understand why she chose to write a book about her.[2]

In an elaboration of her 1976 *Pisces* article, Suzette A. Henke offers "Lillian Beye's Labyrinth: A Freudian Exploration of *Cities of the Interior*" (1984). Henke develops her thesis– that "Lillian embodies the developing ego in its quest for independent self-realization" (113)–through a careful examination of Lillian as she appears in the first and last novels of the *Cities* sequence. Though Henke's terminology is explicitly Freudian, the understanding of Lillian that she arrives at is not significantly different from that discovered by earlier critics. This is not a shortcoming of Henke's approach or application but a consequence of the fact that Nin's texts are self-glossing: any approach to articulating theme will lead to the same conclusion.

Ubiratan Paiva de Oliveira highlights the main features of *Spy* as part of an introductory essay to Nin's work (1985). This author stresses the novel's spatial plan, Nin's adroitness at investing even trivial objects with symbolic suggestiveness, her orchestration of theme-bolstering image clusters, and other matters long familiar to students of Nin's work. In fact, this essay is fully and exclusively, but not richly, dependent on the views of Evans, Hinz, and Balakian.

Though it begins with comment on the short story "Hejda," Catherine Broderick's "The Song of the Womanly Soul: Mask and Revelation in Japanese Literature and in the Fiction of Anaïs Nin" (1986) draws many of its examples from two of the *Cities* novels: *Heart* and *Spy*. Broderick contrasts the Japanese Noh/Buddhist tradition in which "woman's mystery is honored and described through the retained mask" (183) with the debilitating, imprisoning masks worn by Nin's troubled protagonists. Phases of the cultural contrast are highlighted by reference to the works of the Japanese novelist Fumiko Enchi and to Yukio Mishima's *Confessions of a Mask*.

Collages

Nin's career as a fiction writer ended with the publication of *Collages* in 1964, the same year that Swallow published the first American edition of Nin's earliest title, her study of D. H. Lawrence. Reviewers generally address the same mixture of strengths and weaknesses as they had been commenting on for decades. Occasional fine passages may not justify the underdeveloped ideas and characters (John Fuller), the distance from life as it is lived (William Goyen, in a generally positive review), and structural problems that leave one wondering if the work has any point (anonymous "Briefly Noted – Fiction" review in the *New Yorker*). James Korges finds the book marked by incoherent structure and verbal inaccuracies. Elizabeth Jennings praises the book's sustained intensity and considers Renate a convincing character. Like other critics, however, she judges Nin's style somewhat precious and false. In *"Collages* by Anaïs Nin," the anonymous *Los Angeles Free Press* reviewer seems to be a Nin partisan who has read all the earlier rave notices of Nin's fictions and made a collage of accolades. It is one of a small handful of puffs that appeared at the time of publication.

In his chapter-length treatment, Evans notes the heterogeneous nature of the work, suggesting that it "might be more properly described as a collection of short stories with a single common character" (178). Renate, he observes, does not undergo change and is actually a peripheral figure in many of the episodes, some of which have their own interest. Evans outlines the book, praising the "verbal magic" of the Varda episode, making the appropriate thematic connections to Nin's earlier fictions, and commenting appreciatively on the trick circular ending. He considers *Collages* an uneven work that is far weaker than Nin's best. Positive reviews (found more often in British than in American periodicals), he suggests, reflect Nin's delayed recognition as an important writer rather than the actual merits of this book. Nonetheless, he applauds Nin for trying something new.

Called by Hinz "the most satiric and objective" of Nin's writings (61), *Collages* receives no extended discussion by either Hinz or Spencer. Yet Spencer is indebted to this work for her own metaphorical title – *Collage of*

Dreams, and in her introductory chapter, "The Art of Ragpicking," Spencer's discussion of collage technique illuminates Nin's method in this book, taken to be an example in microcosm of the method of Nin's entire fiction enterprise.[3] In a later chapter, "Transforming the Muse," Spencer assesses Renate as "the most fully developed example of Anaïs Nin's concept of feminity and art" (115). Renate is creative and constructive in her relationships with others as well as in her vocation as a painter. She is fluid without being fragmented. Spencer's brief discussion of Renate as an exemplary figure is as compelling as it is astute.

Knapp offers no examination of *Collages*, another curious omission in her eccentric, uneven study. Worse, she misrepresents the nature of the book, calling it "a collection of portraits, short stories, and novellas" (18). Here and elsewhere, Knapp's inaccuracies tend to undermine her rich, empathetic insights.

With the Franklin and Schneider monograph, discussion of *Collages* returns to the high plateau of serious concern first visited by Evans. They point out the many ways in which Nin's final novel is a departure from her earlier ones: the familiar cast of characters has been replaced; there are many more than the usual number of major figures; Renate, the central character, is not a troubled woman in search of wholeness; there is greater geographical movement. They note the discontinuities between many of the sections, questioning the impact of both this feature and the claim of humorous intention on the reader.

The major vignettes receive sustained attention, as does the gradual shift in focus from episodes in which Renate is a participant to those in which she is primarily an observer. Franklin and Schneider do justice to the cyclical design of *Collages* and to the multiple ways of responding to the ending. In particular, they note how it underscores Nin's characteristic concern with the twinned ventures of diary and fiction. As a comic novel, Franklin and Schneider find *Collages* ineffective. "It works best," they maintain, "as a flawed extension of the continuous novel" in which "Renate is merely a weak sister" to Nin's earlier female protagonists (163).

In her "Anaïs Nin" chapter (1981), Sylvia Paine makes some innovative but unconvincing excuses for the limitations of Renate (both as character and as exemplary figure) leveled by Evans and others. In fact, she mounts a full-fledged defense, perceiving an almost ego-less Renate whose empathic powers allow her to merge "her buoyant unconscious" with those stifled by inhibition, "freeing them to act" (90).

Scholar's short chapter on *Collages* is called "We Must Always Smile," a reference to the character Nobuko who forces a smile by pushing up the corners of her mouth. Like Franklin and Schneider, Scholar discovers little humor in the book, though she admits to locating "several delightful interludes." A controlling design, however, is lacking in what Scholar characterizes as "Nin's swan song to her fiction" (127). Scholar praises several of the character sketches; however, she disagrees with Spencer's claim regarding Renate, whom Scholar considers insufficiently developed. She points to the portrait of Varda as one of the few positive representations of a male character in Nin's fiction, and she explores the novel's intriguing last episode, finding echoes of Djuna Barnes's *Nightwood* as well as an imagistic and thematic coda of Nin's fictional *oeuvre*.

Notes to Chapter 5

[1]Probably the most succinct condemnation of *Cities* is found in a single paragraph (284-85) of Andrew Lytle's "Impressionism, the Ego, and the First Person" (1963), a detailed examination of literary impressionism that also considers the work of Henry Miller, Lawrence Durrell, and Djuna Barnes. Addressing *Ladders*, Lytle argues that because the heroine's sacrifice of home, husband, and children has no affective power (for neither home, husband, nor children are made a convincing part of Lillian's awareness), her striving for further fulfillment can only reach the reader as monstrous egoism.

[2] See my "Warring Against Her Partisans" (1986) for more on Scholar's adversarial approach.

[3]This chapter also appears as an essay in Spencer's *Anaïs, Art and Artists*. It had an earlier life as "The Art of Collage in Anaïs Nin's Writing." See also Spencer's entry on Nin in the *Critical Survey of Long Fiction* (1983).

6: Nin's *Diary*

IT SEEMS CERTAIN THAT the original cause of Nin's celebrity, the fabled *Diary* first witnessed and applauded by Henry Miller in the 1930s, will be the foundation of Nin's hold on critics and the reading public for generations to come. Since publication began in 1966, the *Diary* has received far more attention than any of Nin's other efforts. While some have questioned the status of diary and autobiography as literature, Nin's reputation has benefited from a conjunction of forces that has given such forms the imprimaturs once reserved for fiction. One might even suggest that Nin's own achievement has had some influence on the ascendancy of autobiographical writing in the literary pantheon.

In part, the elevated status of journals and diaries has been a consequence of feminist criticism's concern with and attack on the male-determined history of literary standards, including a hierarchy of genres that drew a line shutting journals out (with a few notable exceptions). Defined as an activity particularly if not peculiarly feminine, diary writing had to await the enhanced status and power of women in the literary and academic establishments before it could claim a place of esteem.

Another factor contributing to the elevated position of autobiographical writing (as well as nonfiction writing in general) was the blurring of lines between fiction and nonfiction that become fashionable in the 1960s. Works by Norman Mailer, William Styron, Truman Capote, and other writers established as fiction makers demanded a new kind of attention that diminished the status gap between fiction and nonfiction. "Narratology" became a critical preoccupation that cut across the traditional fiction-nonfiction distinction – or ignored it. Critical interest intensified around the ways in which fictions were autobiographical and the ways in which autobiographies were inventions. In its own way, Nin's critical work of 1968, *The Novel of the Future*, forms part of this discussion.

But Henry Miller had seen it all coming: "it" being not only the esteem that Nin's *Diary* would eventually win her, but also the higher valuing of expositions of the self. For had not Miller, in 1934, found the perfect authority for his own enterprise in Emerson's prophetic utterance, borrowed as epigraph for *Tropic of Cancer*?

> These novels will give way, by and by, to diaries or biographies – captivating books, if only a man knew how to choose among what he calls his experiences that which is really his experience, and how to record truth truly.

Nin's preface to the Paris edition of *Cancer* attends to other matters, but surely these words must have resonated within her.

Published commentary on Nin's diary begins in the ecstasy of Miller's essay "Un Être Étoilique" (1937), surely one of the greatest acts of gallant ry, hustling, and superheated insight that literary history has to offer. Miller writes about the American future from the perspective of the European present, perceiving that the biographical mode is succeeding the "dying forms" of literary art. At the same time, he can claim that the "ellipses of art" exist even in diaries, which have "a form and language as exacting as other literary forms" (6). He states as a general truth that the ultimate goal of the diary is neither beauty nor truth (though both are by-products) but self-realization, and that the quest involves tortuous repetitions of death and rebirth. In the grandest works of the self, like Proust's final volume, "The purely personal, Narcissistic element is resolved into the universal" (7).

Turning to Nin's writing, he observes "this cosmic pulsation" of death and rebirth: "the chaos of regeneration" (8). Summarizing the major narrative threads, Miller traces the key exterior and interior dramas in an excited prose that illuminates Nin's version of the "human document" that "rivals the work of art, or in times such as ours, *replaces* the work of art. For, in a profound sense, this *is* the work of art which never gets written – because the artist whose task it is to create it never gets born" (13).

Miller, in whose own work less was never more, anticipates the objection of over-elaboration, insisting at one and the same time that the "spirit of elaboration" is intrinsic to the form and that the writings of great spirits, however inexhaustible, always leave us wanting more. He recognizes in Nin's work a fresh, feminine evocation of the human experience, a different sense of time, "a blinding, gem-like consciousness which disperses ego like stardust" (22). Indeed, there is little that has been explored in all the years since Miller's encomium that does not have its seed in "Un Être Étoilique."

If there is a sense of distortion, and there is, one must attribute it to two factors. One, Miller is a man in love with his subject in more than the academic meaning of the phrase. Nin the person and Nin the exponent of the exposition of self are still objects of adoration as well as heralds in the design of Miller's exuberant self-love. More importantly, Miller is reacting to manuscript volumes that have not gone through the censorship and the other kinds of editorial reduction and fashioning that preceded publication. What he is writing about few others have yet read.

Another who read Nin's diaries of childhood and early womanhood was Otto Rank. Indeed, during the mid-thirties both Miller and Rank urged Nin to bring a selection of this material to publication, Miller planning to publish it by subscription.[1] To that end, as early as 1935 Rank had prepared a preface (eventually published in 1972 as "Reflections on the Diary of a Child"). Rank reviews the circumstances that led to the creation of the diary, understanding the diary as a remaking of the self that seemed lost upon Nin's abandonment by her father. Rank considers carefully the nature of meeting between father and daughter some twenty years later, connecting this episode to the classic pattern of incest narratives he had explored and written about many years earlier. These narratives, he instructs, are "symbolic representations of cosmic cycles, as myths of the Sun and the Moon which flee and meet each other alternatively" (65). In his observations about the cosmic man and the cosmic woman, Rank anticipates his later formulations regarding a feminine psychology. The value of the diary, for Rank, is its expression of universal mythic patterns from a woman's perspective. He has no concern with formal or stylistic issues.

Although the reading public was kept informed about the legendary diary, and although plans came and went regarding its publication, the mystery and anticipation grew until the appearance, in 1966, of the first volume – a carving representing not the abandoned girl or the newlywed, but the rebellious woman in her late twenties and early thirties awakening *as* a writer. Beginning with this volume, filled with tantalizing stories of Miller, Rank, Artaud, and other intriguing figures, critical response to Nin's life's work has been voluminous and almost nonstop. Nin's partisans and her detractors recognized that with the diary becoming at last the *Diary*, the critical debate over Nin's achievement as a writer had become a high stakes game.

Cutting lists thirty-four reviews of *Diary* 1 published in 1966; no doubt there were many more. Not only was a work by Nin receiving more immediate attention than any previous Nin title, but this work was also receiving a higher proportion of positive responses. Most persuasive is Karl Shapiro's "The Charmed Circle of Anaïs Nin" in which Nin is praised for having developed a new form that blends "the charm of authenticity" with "the full dimensions of the novel." Detractors, however, remain numerous and forceful. These include Bernard Benstock, who uses Nin's comments about writing to assert: "The literature of Anaïs Nin (and her diary tells us why) remains all tendrils and membranes, and three layers of skin – no bones and no flesh" (804). Less hostile, though certainly not enthusiastic, is Leon Edel's "Life Without Father." Edel appreciates the volume for its portrait of an era and especially of Otto Rank, fastens on its major themes, and neatly sets Nin and her esthetic into "that last backwater of Romanticism before World War II."

With the appearance of *Diary* 2 the following year, reviewers are pressed to make generalizations about this ongoing publishing enterprise, but the early overviews do not hold up because the several volumes have diverse characteristics. By the time the cycle of seven volumes comes to an end, a consensus emerges that the literary, biographical, and cultural interest is strongest in the first two Paris-centered volumes, slightly less intense in volumes three and four focused on Nin's struggles and successes in New York. The later volumes seem to reflect a changed role for the *Diary* in Nin's life – a thinning of commitment. However, in his "Portrait of the Artist as Diarist" (1974), William Goyen considers volume five "the most unified and shapely" of the volumes published to date. Only Nin's most devoted followers have much enthusiasm for *Diary* 7 (completed for publication after Nin's death and vigorously attacked by James Wolcott in his 1980 review "Life Among the Ninnies"), and many readers observe the tendency for successive volumes to treat longer spans of time in fewer pages. During and after the fifteen-year period of its publication, investigations of the *Diary* as a problem in genre grow more lively and complex, especially as critics come to consider Nin's editorial habits and Gunther Stuhlmann's role in the editing process.

It is not long before the arena of discussion shifts from the popular review media to the academic periodicals and monographs. In his *Anaïs Nin* (1968), Oliver Evans places his chapter on the *Diary* just after his brief introduction and before his treatment of Nin's fictions, which he discusses in the order of their publication. It is probable that Evans was well along the way to completing his study of Nin's fiction when the first *Diary* volumes were planned for publication, making some discussion of them obligatory. However, his quotations bear no page references because his source for quotations was the manuscript diary. For Evans, then, the *Diary* is not yet a book or series of books. In a note, Evans observes that his discussion "is limited to the first volume of the *Diary*, that is, the portion covering the period from 1931 to 1936" (199). *Diary* 1 actually covers 1931-34. Evans may have worked from a state of the diary at some point in the process of its preparation for publication and not had the time or inclination to revise following the appearances of the first two volumes in 1966 and 1967 (items acknowledged in the preface by Harry T. Moore).

Whatever the case, Evans's chapter title, "Genesis of a Fiction: The Diary," properly labels his orientation. For him, Nin's *Diary* is less important in itself than as the source of materials for the short stories and novels. His aim is to provide glimpses of the creative process, to illustrate the relationships between passages in Nin's published fictions and their origins. He points to the ideas, obsessions, characters, events, images, and symbols that find their way from diary to fiction. He also outlines Rank's influence on Nin's attitude toward the diary and toward herself as an artist, paying special attention to her growing interest in dreams. His emphasis, then, is on the diary as writer's workbook, though he also insists that it has great historical value as a record the Parisian bohemian milieu in the early thirties. He takes no position on it as an artwork. In fact, he goes so far as to say that "the focus of [Nin's] attention in the Diary is now [during the mid sixties] where, for a novelist, it belongs: on the potential characters of her fiction" (8). Of the other book-length studies, those by Knapp and Scholar also treat the *Diary* first, but to somewhat different purpose and effect.

Nin's first *Diary* volume caught the attention of Mary Ellmann, whose widely praised *Thinking About Women* (1968) explores the range and consequences of feminine stereotypes. Ellmann finds in Nin's writing exemplification of how certain female authors' "self-deceptive vanity" leads to a reproduction of age-old stereotypes of women from which the author considers herself an exception. Ellmann also notes how Nin sometimes transfers feminine stereotypes to men (188-91).

Bearing an issue date of 1968, but a copyright date of 1969, is a special number of *Studies in the Twentieth Century* offering three essays on Nin's *Diary*. Daniel Stern's "The Diary of Anaïs Nin" considers the first two volumes as a healthy solution to the dead ends of the non-fiction novel on the one hand and the excesses of literary surrealism on the other. He finds these volumes to be "landmarks in the century's struggle to deal with its experience and its art" (40). Stern emphasizes the thematic tensions – dream versus reality, inner versus outer – and he understands them finally as a "struggle of two styles" (42) that Nin manages to hold in effective balance. He applauds a courageous achievement that does not ask for the abandonment of either reality or fantasy in life or art.

Marianne Hauser's "Anaïs Nin: Myth and Reality" also addresses the first two volumes together. Hauser reviews the mythical status of the *Diary* and Nin's redemption as an artist with its publication. The uniqueness of Nin's achievement lies, for Hauser, in a special combination of features: her multi-cultural perspective, the aura of discovery in her flexible and lucid prose, the fluxuous sense of time, the universal appeal of her personal hunger for perfection and approval, her alertness to the dramatic moment, the rich cast of characters, and the life or personhood she gives to the *Diary* itself.

In his "Portrait of Anaïs Nin as a Bodhisattva: Reflections on the *Diary, 1934-39*," Wayne McEvilly observes that the fragments of Nin's enormous work that are presented to the public have as their broad theme the human psyche, a theme advanced through various sub-themes that are related much as musical themes are related in a Bach fugue. For McEvilly, Nin's way of knowing parallels that of the Zen masters, people awakened to the holistic nature of existence. When a person of such insight draws a self-portrait, everything is in it, thus it becomes a piece of wisdom literature. McEvilly's analogy to Eastern philosophy anticipates the invocation of the karma principle in Evelyn J. Hinz's study. In the subsections titled "Music" and "Weaving," McEvilly enthuses over Nin's fluid orchestration of her materials and her ability to transform, through the power of the symbol, the myriad phenomena of outer and inner life into a verbal tapestry of revealed significance. As my characterization may suggest, McEvilly's essay reads much like a passage of Nin's own poetic prose.

In 1970, Hauser once again comments on Nin's *Diary*. "Thoughts on *The Diary of Anaïs Nin*" is an enthusiast's appreciation of the first three volumes. Hauser observes an "upward movement" or "rising curve" of excitement and suspense as Nin shapes the story of her development as woman and artist. One can argue with Hauser's claim that "events are recorded without any trace of self-consciousness" while feeling less insulted by her observations on how "the *Diary* fuses reality, myth, and dream into one shimmering fabric" (64).

It is a mild inconsistency that after treating Nin's variously-titled works of shorter and longer fiction as a single body of work best explored through a plan determined by methods and themes, Evelyn J. Hinz (in *The Mirror and the Garden*, 1971, rev. 1973) develops her discussion of the *Diary*, more legitimately a single, continuous work, by treating it volume by volume. Hinz's approach is partly redeemed by her assertion that the *Diary* has "a historical dimension" (97) and also by the fact that the functions the *Diary* serves (and thus its very character) undergo important if incremental changes.

In her discussion of the *Diary*, Hinz makes her most emphatic and lucid analysis of the interrelationship – as once practical, theoretical, and psychological – between the *Diary* and the fiction. Drawing upon Nin's *The Novel of the Future*, Hinz defends and sharpens Nin's distinctions, distinctions that stress the organicism of the *Diary* and the fixity of traditional fiction. At one time troubled by the conflicting claims of the two modes and by the belief that she had to choose one over the other, Nin came to accept their potential for a harmonious interdependence.

Hinz provides discussions of about four pages in length for each of the first four volumes (two volumes in the first edition). For each, she offers a succinct interpretive summary that describes its focus as a stage in Nin's odyssey of self. Thus, volume 1 shows us Nin's birth as an artist, thinker, and independent woman; volume 2 elaborates "the question of the public responsibility of the artist" (105); volume 3 has cultural contrast as a central theme; the fourth volume shows Nin emerging as a writer with a public, struggling with the opinions of critics and with the responsibilities of mentorship and symbolic motherhood to new, usually young, disciples.[2]

In characterizing the separate volumes, Hinz is alert to the editorial hand (Nin's) at work, reshaping the manuscript diary material in ways that raise questions of genre, sincerity, and authenticity, but she chooses not to explore these issues. In contrast to Evans, Hinz treats the *Diary* after treating the fiction – an arrangement followed by Sharon Spencer as well as by Franklin and Schneider.

Essays on Nin's *Diary* reach flood stage in the early seventies, even while more volumes are coming into print. Wayne McEvilly once again explores the affinities between Nin's *Diary* and Eastern thought in his elegant and eclectic "The Bread of Tradition: Reflections on the Diary of Anaïs Nin" (1971). Only McEvilly could think of a way to compare Nin to Laurence Sterne. Again, he honors the *Diary* as a most profound piece of wisdom literature, bread for the spirit. Ann Snitow, in "Women's Private Writings: Anaïs Nin" (also 1971) contrasts Nin's 1930s brand of feminine consciousness with the feminist consciousness of her admiring and/or critical readers of the 1960s and 1970s. Snitow wonders why women tend to choose private modes for their most important writing and hazards some guesses in response to Nin's practice and attitudes toward her diary. Patricia Meyer Spacks, in her speculation on "Free Women" (1971-72) considers Nin's case as revealed in the *Diary* alongside of autobiographical writings by Lillian Hellman and Doris Lessing. Spacks finds common threads in these writers' obsessive scrutinies of freedom's psychic and social limitations for women.

The theme of Nin as "a champion of omission" inspires the *TLS* review of *Diary* 4, "Not to Need, but To Be Needed" (1972). This review is important as an early indication of critics' concerns with the editorial roles of Nin and Stuhlmann, with unanswered questions raised by suppressed information, and with inconsistent execution of the stated policy of respecting personal privacy. The reviewer finds Nin praiseworthy as a self-realizing force, but "untalented" as a writer.

Two essays of 1973 compare and contrast Nin's *Diary* with writings by Doris Lessing. Sharon Spencer's " 'Femininity' and the Woman Writer: Doris Lessing's *The Golden Notebook* and the *Diary* of Anaïs Nin" concerns itself with these writers' revelations of "conflict between the woman artist's personal individualized sense of identity and her biologically conditioned role" (249). For Spencer, both works are valuable for their detailed presentations of how woman writers came to accept "the male principle within themselves" without denying or "making a fetish" of their femininity (252). The pole for comparison in Catharine R. Stimpson's "Authority and Absence: Women Write on Men" is Lessing's fiction sequence, *Children of Violence*. Stimpson enumerates the strategies by which Nin and Lessing explore women's consciousness as it considers men and masculinity, noting the absence of feminist strategies. Outlining what she calls Nin's ideology of gender, Stimpson notes how Nin's "ideological fix" affects her comments about male homosexuals (85). She points out the similarity in how both authors address women's lies, especially those lies that sustain male self-esteem and how both "pay homage to the masculine figure who radiates a benign authority: the good father" (90).

Robert Zaller's *A Casebook on Anaïs Nin* (1974) provides six essays on Nin's *Diary* which, along with an interview by Priscilla English and a misplaced general assessment by Lynn Sukenick, constitute the third part of this collection. Some of these titles first appeared in periodicals, while others were written especially for this project. They are all adulatory, as the admitted intention of Zaller's project is to make a case (his pun) for Nin. Deena Metzger's "The *Diary*: The Ceremony of Knowing" is an example of school-of-beauties criticism; it is a pastiche of quotations with breathy links about how much Nin's work means to her readers. Rambling through the first five volumes, Metzger attempts a creative, responsive criticism that results only in earnest bursts of cheerleading. Diane Wakoski's "A Tribute to

Anaïs Nin" blends its enthusiasm with a clear, graceful style and a tighter focus. Wakoski's testimony is to the inspiring fascination Nin brings to woman artists by way of her self-portrait. Nin's originality in her seeming obliteration of the boundary between life and art is liberating, opening "a whole new world for all of us writing today" (150).

Daniel Stern's "The Novel of Her Life: *The Diary of Anaïs Nin, Volume IV, 1944-1947*" is informed, responsible review criticism that observes the central themes of the earlier volumes while claiming the new installment to be "a self-contained historical novel" (155) that delineates New York and America "preparing itself for the postwar world" (154). Stern enjoys the way in which Nin's story winds through and captures the lives of others, especially influential figures like Gore Vidal and Edmund Wilson. Nin's style and sensibility, however, take both the famous and the obscure out of time – she gives them the permanence of "characters."

In "Anaïs Nin's *Diary I*: The Birth of the Young Woman as an Artist," Tristine Rainer essentially retells the story that Nin tells in large. However, Rainer contributes to our sense of Nin's artistry by drawing attention to how characters and places take on polar significances that clarify the tensions Nin experienced during this period. Many of these polarities represent the choice between death and life, convention and liberation, that Nin must make over and over again.

Even more probing is Richard R. Centing's "Emotional Algebra: The Symbolic Level of *The Diary of Anaïs Nin, 1944-1947.*" He sees this volume as a microcosm of Nin's symbolic world, a world delineated through notational schemes involving colors, descriptions of eyes, and references to size and to water. Centing wishes to shift the grounds for discussing Nin's *Diary* from who she is to how she writes, from the particulars in history to the particulars in vision. He has some success, particularly noticeable among the company he keeps here, toward achieving his end.

Zaller's own "Anaïs Nin and the Truth of Feeling" is one more ode to Nin's concern with "protecting her own humanity in order to extend it to others" (179). Gathering some of the proportionally tiny number of *Diary* references to the public/political world into his essay, Zaller testifies to the worthiness of Nin's withdrawal from that terrible business into a relatively private, personal life intensely lived and scrutinized and registered. The *Diary* shows her as an exemplary instrument of fine responsiveness: Saint Anaïs of Her Own Feelings.

During the winter of 1974-1975, portions of Margaret Lee Potts's dissertation were published as "The Genesis and Evolution of the Creative Personality: A Rankian Analysis of *The Diary of Anaïs Nin.*" Nin's *Diary*, Potts demonstrates, is "an embodiment of creative genesis and evolution" (6) sharing the assumptions of and enacting the pattern described in Rank's theories of personal growth and of the artistic personality. Though Nin's emphasis often varies from Rank's, the drama of the self enacted in the early *Diary* volumes echoes the formulations of Rank's *Art and Artist* almost as if Nin had found the blueprint for her edifice in that seminal work. The materials excerpted from Potts's third chapter on the process of self-nomination and identification are particularly useful, including her formulations regarding the importance of Nin's book on D. H. Lawrence to that process.

Lynn Sukenick's "The *Diaries* of Anaïs Nin" (1976) is certainly one of the most attractive and intelligent appreciations of Nin's unique enterprise, an artwork which is neither journal nor novel but a special kind of autobiographical mode. Sukenick is alert to the standard criticisms regarding inauthenticity, but argues that "Nin's power . . . is not a direct function of how much she tells us" (97) and that the *Diary's* characteristic distillations of experience and style are appropriate creative gestures of the very personality being revealed. Furthermore, Sukenick argues that these polished distillations create a mirrored surface in which readers can find themselves. Nin's acts of discretion are in the service of possibility and transformation. Her work is not, finally, confessional. Her frank refusal to share everything may be preferable to "the confession which accidentally or deliberately conceals" (103). For Sukenick, Nin's message is that the habits of mind through which we traditionally define ourselves, and upon which literary realism depends, are infected with the dross and trivia of our lives. She would have us see ourselves and make ourselves anew.

Originally published in *Le Monde* in 1976 as "Portrait de l'Artiste en Femme," Kate Millett's "Anaïs – A Mother to Us All: The Birth of the Artist as a Woman" is a reminder that at least one prominent feminist finds Nin's achievement significant. Millett tells her audience that of all the woman writers who had risen to prominence after World War II, Nin is the one who has come to matter most to the women's movement. And the *Diary* is specifically what matters: as a new form, as the expression of a sensibility of "exquisite discernment," and as a personal record of every woman's struggle. "We are the future she has made possible," writes Millett, "and the past accepted, transcended, embraced" (8).

In her *Collage of Dreams* (1977; 1981), Sharon Spencer pushes the exploration of genre initiated by Hinz and taken up by Sukenick a bit further while arguing that the *Diary* is more authentic for its departures from the life lived: "Nin's Diary is a more authentic, certainly a more complete, deeper, and fuller expression of her self than the actual life she has lived" (126). And later, "Anaïs Nin is, in a crucial sense, herself plus the Diary in which she has recorded an amazing number and variety of unlived as well as lived selves" (129). As ever, Spencer is skillful at putting a positive complexion on troublesome aspects of Nin's art. At the same time, her formulations reveal the difficulty of setting one's critical focus solely on either (1) *Diary* as artwork, or (2) Nin as historical personage.

Spencer provides two chapters on the *Diary*. The first, "Anaïs: Her Book," takes up the question of identity – the relationship between Nin as author and Nin as subject – and at the same time reviews succinctly the centers of interest in the separate volumes.[3] In making these characterizations, Spencer sometimes echoes and sometimes sets up contrasts with Hinz's perspectives. For example, for Spencer the theme of the third volume is loss. The second chapter, "The 'Journal des Autres,' " examines parallels between the *Diary* and Proust's autobiographical fiction, *Remembrance of Things Past*. In this chapter, Spencer underscores the ways in which Nin's *Diary* engages the reader in the very processes of consciousness and self-meditation that create it as well as more traditional artworks. Spencer is also concerned with how, in Nin's life writing, the private becomes universal. Through the comparison with Proust, Spencer helps dissipate the concern with the limits of genre.

Love, relationship, and creation are found by Jean Bradford to be the motifs of Nin's first six diary volumes. In "The Self: A Mosaic, A Loving Perspective on the Diaries of Anaïs Nin" (1977), Bradford touches briefly upon each volume, putting into focus the way each elaborates these motifs. Bradford stresses Nin's gradual opening, the movement from vulnerability to a liberated sharing of the self. The published *Diary* is one aspect of that sharing, and it can serve as spiritual nourishment for others who need to take a similar journey. Bradford is more concerned with the *Diary* as a prototype of therapy than as art.

Knapp devotes the first chapter of her *Anaïs Nin* (1978) to examining the *Diary* as a sourcebook for Nin's ideas and for those events in her life that constitute the raw material of her fiction. Indeed, she builds her biographical introduction from that source and at the same time abstracts it. Concerned with Nin as a fiction writer, Knapp provides no keys to the literary significance of the *Diary*, treating it even less searchingly than Evans had even though she concluded her study ten years later with the first six volumes in print. Because she offers no explanation for this perfunctory and superficial discussion and barely mentions the *Diary* thereafter, Knapp undercuts the utility of her study and makes it, if for no other reason, the least satisfactory of the six monographs.

Four essays on Nin's *Diary* appear in Evelyn J. Hinz's collection, *The World of Anaïs Nin* (1978), a special issue of *Mosaic*. In "Archetypal Constellations of Feminine Consciousness in Nin's First *Diary*," Stephanie A. Demetrakopoulos provides a modified Jungian reading in which she discovers an underlying structure of archetypes raised to Nin's consciousness for the purposes of control and understanding. In Jungian nomenclature, Nin as mistress of revealing her life's ceremonies is an "Introverted Artemis" personality. The revelations themselves present her as Persephone, Demeter, Venus, Hestia, and others. Other people fashioned or refashioned in the *Diary* also play out archetypal roles. In this lucid and patiently argued analysis, Demetrakopoulos puts a theory of the human psyche and of human creativity in the service of elucidation, but never forces the *Diary* into a jacket that will not fit. She is concerned both with what Nin's writing confirms and does not confirm regarding theories of the psyche and its growth.

Catherine Broderick's "Anaïs Nin's *Diary* and the Japanese Literary Diary Tradition" provides a highly specialized focus, yet one that is fruitful in assisting our perception of Nin's purpose and achievement. After tracing the history of the Japanese literary diary, Broderick surveys some of its characteristics and their cultural implications including the acceptance of "the validity of inner or psychological experience" (182). Nin's reception in Japan, and particularly that of the *Diary*, is related, Broderick argues, to different attitudes toward and expectations of autobiographical writing stemming from different perceptions of truthfulness, of the importance of the self, and in notions of constitutes literariness.

"Anaïs Nin's *Diary* in Context," by Lynn Z. Bloom and Orlee Holder, strives to develop a working, illustrated definition of feminine autobiographical writing that will serve as a grid on which to locate and assess Nin's achievement. Reviewing the critical theory in this field as well as the primary texts, Bloom and Holder approach Nin's *Diary* both as a member of a family and as a somewhat independent stranger in its midst. Nin's work shares with the family such features as "structural discontinuity and pervasive thematic concerns" including the writing life, maturation struggles, and a multiplicity of roles or identities. Nin's *Diary* steps outside of the family circle in its polish and formality. Also, though it is not conventionally structured in ways that promote unity and coherence, it nevertheless leaves the reader with a sense of a cohesive, whole fabric.

The most provocative and challenging of the *Mosaic* essays is Duane Schneider's "Anaïs Nin in the *Diary*: The Creation and Development of a Persona." Schneider traces the incremental shifts in the Nin persona from "conventional literary heroine" as she makes her entrance to a "most humanely realized and most fully human" controlling consciousness in the sixth volume (19). Throughout, Schneider insists that this narrator is a literary creation, a character Nin to be confused by Nin and yet testimony to Nin's artistic (including her editorial) skill.

Schneider's approach is elaborated in the nearly 100-page section by Benjamin Franklin V and Schneider in their *Anaïs Nin: An Introduction* (1979). This discussion constitutes the second of the three parts of their book, the first given over to the fiction and the third to Nin's "Criticism and Nonfiction." Thus structurally and proportionally, engagement with the *Diary* (through volume 6) takes up one-third of this study.[4]

Franklin and Schneider are the first to explore questions of authority and genre in detail. Though they stop short of presenting solutions, they articulate the problems forcefully. The distinction between manuscript diary and multi-volume *Diary* is a distinction they insist all readers and critics keep in mind. To characterize the one is not to characterize the other. The issues they outline are (1) editorial responsibility and its consequences, (2) generic character: is it journal or autobiography as a "consciously structured, rearranged" series of volumes, and (3) "the function of time, composition, and organization on the finished product" (169).

Each of these issues is patiently explored, though – as the authors readily admit – much of the desired evidence is not available. With respect to the genre issue, Franklin and Schneider suggest that the *Diary*, whatever its degree of faithfulness to parts of the original manuscript, is best considered as "a newly created work of art" that matches and often surpasses Nin's fiction as literature "because it is rooted more firmly in an identifiable and substantial context" (172). Thus they have urged us to see the uniqueness of the *Diary*, closer to retrospective autobiography than to journal, but not quite or not only autobiography either.

In discussing the third issue, Franklin and Schneider hypothesize about the process by which the "journal-letter" became a "journal-novel" (176). Their discussion here is particularly useful in reminding us that the poised and practiced novelist of the 1960s – *that* Anaïs Nin – was not quite the same person who had written the manuscript diaries of some thirty-five years earlier. As an editor, Nin worked with enhanced skills; as an autobiographer, she filtered events through memory even while drawing upon the manuscripts. And, as the first *Diary* volumes brought Nin long-delayed acceptance, her approach to the presentation of self in succeeding volumes may have shifted.

Each of the first six volumes receives a separate chapter in which Franklin and Schneider summarize the encounters of the "narrator/persona" in Nin's "real continuous novel" (186). Addressing themes manifest through dramatically rendered relationships, the authors keep in mind the concerns regarding genre and authority raised earlier. They also make precise comparative judgments on the success of the individual volumes as artworks, noting especially differences in unity, coherence, and intensity. The general pattern that Franklin and Schneider observe is one of diminishment of focus from the high achievement of the first volume (though the second is almost as admirable) through the fifth, with a reassertion of powerful sense of the whole in volume 6. Each volume, however, includes segments or passages of great impact and artistry.

In "Anaïs Nin: A Freudian Perspective" (1980), Suzette Henke offers a series of fascinating speculations regarding Nin's attitude toward her girlish physique, her flirtation with Dr. Allendy, and her editorial habit of suppressing references to negative and threatening feelings. "The Freudian analyst," Henke suggests, "might interpret Nin's careful construction of an 'ego ideal' as a narcissistic project to re-establish infant omnipotence" (12).

Albert E. Stone's "Becoming a Woman in Male America: Margaret Mead and Anaïs Nin" (1982) examines Nin's *Diary* less as a strictly literary enterprise and more as a "cultural narrative" showing a woman's "fight for an authentic feminine identity" (197). Particularly interested in Nin's reconstructive editorial act that remakes the diary into autobiography, Stone argues that Nin has the goal of uniting "conscious art and spontaneous life" (211) while at the same time reinventing the female self in a man's world. Stone is especially alert to the symbolic weight of Nin's portraits of others, and he derives useful insights from the unexpected comparison of the *Diary* to Mead's *Blackberry Winter*. Indeed, he establishes an important place for Nin's work in the larger context of modern American women autobiographers, a context that allows for as much insight into her achievement as the conventional, Nin-inspired yoking with Proust. Stone carefully links the issue of genre with that of gender.

One of the best rejoinders to the approach taken by Lynn Sukenick is Joan Bobbitt's "Truth and Artistry in the *Diary of Anaïs Nin*" (1982). Bobbitt argues that the "calculated artistry" of the *Diary* stands "in direct opposition to Nin's espoused ideal of naturalness and spontaneity" (267). Ostensibly about the evolution of the self, the self-portrait that emerges is embarrassingly static. It is astonishing to Bobbitt that Nin invests so much in the claim of frankness while simultaneously undermining the bond of trust between writer and reader. Nin's theoretical celebration of the sensual is never matched by the compelling testimony of personal experience. While building the myth of herself as an archetypal mother, Nin glosses over the experience of her pregnancy as if it made no impact on her (except for the set piece on the stillbirth). For Bobbitt, Nin has kept herself well-hidden, only presenting in the *Diary* those materials that "affirm her masks and personal fictions" (276).

Concise yet provocative is Margaret Miller's "Seduction and Subversion in *The Diary of Anaïs Nin*" (1983), which probes the conflicting impulses of secrecy and exposure, serving and controlling, that manifest themselves so strongly in the first three volumes. Miller unravels Nin's struggles with the attitudes of Henry Miller and Otto Rank toward the diary, and with her own ambivalence regarding its dual – private/public – nature. By generating her own massive myth into which the major male figures in her life are absorbed, Nin ultimately escapes the limited self or selves imposed on her by her father, by Miller, and by Rank.

Some of the concerns briefly explored by Margaret Miller and Joan Bobbitt are developed more fully in the harsh light of Nancy Scholar's critique. Two chapters of her *Anaïs Nin* (1984) are given over to the *Diary*, which she treats ahead of the fiction. The first, "The Diaries: The Art of Seduction," examines Nin's *Diary* as an ongoing act of self-creation. Scholar understands Nin's production of "a mythological version of self" as an exaggerated version of a tendency shared by all autobiographical projects, one that necessitates fitting "all the pieces into the appropriate legendary shape" (15). Scholar is critical of Nin's editorial habits, finding Nin constantly self-justifying and yet conveniently reticent on matters that might undermine the legend. She does not accept, for example, Nin's explanation for omitting mention of her husband in the first round of *Diary* volumes, finding this omission consistent with Nin's aim of fabricating the idealized Anaïs, "a courageous, independent woman struggling to forge her own identity and art" (21).

One form of seduction is what Scholar calls "the art of sincerity" (26). Nin has seduced first herself, and by extension her readers, with a work labeled *Diary* that is hardly a diary at all. Nin's art of sincerity traps the reader into an uncritical response. Thankful for Nin's supposed directness and trust, the reader is predisposed to approve. Flattered by being given access to what was undertaken in private, the reader is seduced with privilege. By claiming that the *Diary* is not art but life, Nin forestalls objections on artistic grounds. Yet there is abundant evidence that Nin imagined the *Diary* as a public work in the 1930s, and there is overwhelming evidence of Nin's artful superimpositions upon the original manuscript diaries. For Scholar, as for Bobbitt, Nin's art of sincerity is compromised in many ways.

Scholar's next chapter, "The Diaries: Mirrors and Windows," attends to Nin's focus on the inner life and to her attempts at universalizing the personal. Her judgment is that "ultimately [Nin's] Diary fails to be the monumental work Miller predicted it would be because it does not maintain a balance between the mirror and the window, between interior and exterior worlds" (44-45). The subjective perspective is overbearing and debilitating; Nin's presentation of her persona as a reflecting psyche undermines the possibility of "a tangible identity" (53). Furthermore, the mirror enhances or distorts in ways that tell us more about the needs of the author and of the *Diary* itself than they do about the other personages involved. Scholar agrees with other critics that the first two *Diary* volumes are the most successful.[5] In fact, she considers these to be Nin's finest works of art, outdistancing the fiction. However, Scholar judges the whole enterprise, especially the later volumes, as compromised by Nin's incessant narcissism and obsessive concern with appearances.

The 1985 issue of *Anaïs* includes a special section on "Writing a Dairy" that features a number of essays on the uses and processes of diary writing. Though all of the discussions are inspired by Nin's practice, only Margaret Miller's "Diary-Keeping and the Young Wife" explores Nin's work directly. Miller considers how volume 3 of *The Early Diary of Anaïs Nin* shows Nin modifying the functions of her diary "to meet the needs of a woman who has just become a wife" (39). Nin copes with the stress of conflict brought by marriage, in her case a conflict between the ideal of the good wife and the reality of the strong-willed young woman whose drive toward self-realization carries her away from an easy compliance with the conventional patterns of wifehood. Miller finds the tensions in this journal predictive of the patterns found in *Diary* volumes for later periods.

In that same issue (but placed outside of the special section) is Dennis R. Miller's "Glimpsing a Goddess – Some Thoughts on the Final Diary."

Miller comments on the ironies in volume 7 of Nin's *Diary*: the acceptance and acclaim that she had so long sought have arrived, but along with the rewards come new responsibilities and sufferings. As a symbolic figure, she becomes something of a slave to devotees who depend on her for strength in spite of her constant message of self-determination. Miller extracts from this last volume a sympathetic portrait of Nin's flawed saintliness.

Like Margaret Miller's piece mentioned above, Anna Balakian's "Anaïs Nin and Feminism" (1986) addresses volume 3 of the *Early Diary*. Balakian shows how Nin's portrait of her "perfect husband" only underscores the problem of finding an individual identity within the structure of a conventionally-defined marriage. Nin's dissatisfaction and rebellion is not entirely rooted in gender issues; rather, it is a rebellion against the shackles of middle-class values shared by artists and intellectuals regardless of sex. Those who see a "rudimentary feminism" in Nin's self-portrait may be back-reading from the perspective of Nin's later proclamations and from their exposure to the women's movement. Nonetheless, with her portrait of Hugh Guiler in "the heroic role of the generous husband" (33), Nin clarified the issue of creating productive relationships in the age of woman's intellectual liberation.

Marie-Claire Van der Elst's "The Birth of a Vocation" (1986) draws upon interviews and passages in both the *Diary* and the *Early Diary* to determine the genesis of Nin's literary vocation. Van der Elst marks Nin's disillusionment with religion as the starting point for a second and transforming commitment to writing. Nin's decision to write in English rather than French is part of the transformation.

In "The Poetry of Experience" (1986), Nancy Jo Hoy offers a middle term, "faithfulness," to describe Nin's objective in writing, editing, and bringing the *Diary* to publication. Lying somewhere between truth and fiction, but not quite offering either, Nin's effort is faithful "to the integrity of events and feelings" (54) in spite of suppressions, distortions of time, and novelistic heightenings. Hoy traces the major themes through the several volumes, labeling them "the assertion of selfhood, the quest for female identity and the conflict between the woman's role and the pursuit of the creative will" (58). Hoy's assessment is similar to Sukenick's in that it recognizes limitations to Nin's achievement in the *Diary* while clarifying its sources of strength. Both value what Hoy calls Nin's "refusal to accept the cultural mythos of objectivity and rational behavior" (66) and her trust in the unconscious as a creative source.

In contrast to the treatment of it in her book, Bettina L. Knapp's appraisal of the *Diary* in "The Diary as Art: Anaïs Nin, Thornton Wilder, Edmund Wilson" (1987) recognizes Nin's *Diary* not merely as a personal document and sourcebook for the fiction but as an independent artwork in its own right. For Knapp, the *Diary* became an artwork when the manuscript underwent a "transformation ritual" (224) that involved the application of a full range of literary techniques upon the original, changing its function and nature. The contrasts Knapp establishes between Nin's work and those of Wilder and Wilson serve to illuminate the special character of each as well as the range of possibilities within the diary mode.

Nin's *Diary* receives brief but significant mention in Susan Stanford Friedman's "Women's Autobiographical Selves: Theory and Practice" (1988). Friedman draws upon the theoretical discussions of Sheila Row-bothom and Nancy Chodorow to explore and explain various features of the feminine consciousness in autobiographical writings that Nin's work reveals. One of these features is "Nin's sense of herself as simultaneously singular and collective, particular and symbolic," a perception Friedman connects to Rowbothom's discussion of the female collective unconscious. Nin's formulation regarding a "fluid, relational self anticipates Chodorow's concept of women's 'more flexible or permeable ego boundaries' " (45)[6]

The 1988 number of *Anaïs: An International Journal* once again features a range of comment on Nin's *Diary*. Doris Niemeyer's "How to Be a Woman and/or an Artist: The Diary as an Instrument of Self-Therapy" (translated by Gunther Stuhlmann) covers much old ground but is useful in its focus on Nin's successive periods of therapy with Allendy, Rank, and Jaeger. In each period, the diary plays an essential role – sometimes in harmony and sometimes in conflict with the dynamics of the analyst-patient relationship. Life without the diary, until late in Nin's career, is life with important aspects of her identity denied. The diary often serves as retreat, a realm of creative expression and introspection where Nin can blunt, if not resolve, the various conflicts of her outer life.

In the same issue, Marie-Line Pétrequin's "The Magic Spell of June Miller: On the Literary Creation of Female Identity in Anaïs Nin's *Diary*" (also translated by Stuhlmann) traces the impact of Henry Miller's second wife on Nin's notions of femininity and explores how the real-life personage is transformed by Nin into a symbolic aspect of feminine possibility. June comes to represent the non-analytical, the sensual, the brazenly independent. Yet June, for all of her refusal to be defined by others, is incapable of choosing or bringing into being an integrated self. Thus her rebellion, as Nin envisions it, is only a limited success. Pétrequin's analysis always keeps in view the role of June Miller, or rather Nin's version of her, in Nin's own developing sense of self through flux of identification and difference.

Nin's relationships with June and Henry Miller, partially disguised by an editorial cloak of mystification in *Diary* 1, became more fully revealed with the publication of *Henry and June* (1986). At the same time, this publication complicated while it illustrated the problem of assessing Nin's achievement as diarist-autobiographer. Rupert Pole's shaping of materials "from the unexpurgated diary" presents not only another side of Nin but also another literary text. Three reactions to this text also appear in the 1988 issue of *Anaïs*. Karin Struck's "Logbook of a Liberation" (translated by Stuhlmann) shows how Nin's dedication to keeping the record of her sensual awakening feeds her development as a writer.[7] Meryle Secrest's "Economics and the Need for Revenge" stresses the pressure of economic enslavement which, though barely mentioned, must have been a contributing factor in Nin's balancing act of her own feelings and behavior toward her husband and Miller. My own "Dropping Another Veil" appraises the text as narrative art, ranking it as high as anything in the Nin canon. However, as a resolving factor in the search for the real Anaïs, I insist that this artful carving does not quite work. It only points up the futility of the search while sharpening one's sense of how the long history of bringing sections of Nin's diary to the public has carried along with it an intriguing and oftimes maddening set of puzzles regarding genre, authority, responsibility, and authenticity.[8]

In "Anaïs Nin's Mothering Metaphor: Toward a Lacanian Theory of Feminine Creativity" (1989), Diane Richard-Allerdyce contends that Nin intuitively reached understandings about language and gender that parallel and are illuminated by the teachings of Jacques Lacan. Nin's formulations in the *Diary* suggest that feminine perspective and identity are more closely associated with unconscious truth than the masculine, and Richard-Allerdyce, after insisting that the primary signifier of gender in this discussion is not biological difference but rather societal or ideational positioning in relation to a God concept, develops a reading of Lacan that harmonizes Nin's insights with Lacan's theory of gender. Lacan, she argues, links femininity and mysticism in ways that can be connected to Nin's concept of feminine creativity. Furthermore, Nin's use of "biological mothering as a metaphor for feminine creativity" (96) is illuminated by the Lacanian concept of metaphor that links biological and metaphorical reproduction. Students of Nin's *Diary* may be left wondering if the candlepower of this illumination is high enough to shine through the filters of critical jargon.

Less threatening is Lori A. Wood's "Between Creation and Destruction: Toward a New Concept of the Female Artist" (1990). Exploring the first two *Diary* volumes as well as *Henry and June*, Wood argues that June Miller "serves as the symbolic vehicle through which Nin eventually reassimilates" the destructive "aspect of the feminine," an aspect necessary for Nin's more fully developed thinking about "the feminine process of creation" (15). Wood maps the shifts in Nin's thinking about the destructive element, noting in particular the influence of Dr. Martha Jaeger and drawing upon the writings of Esther Harding. During a later period, Gonzalo More became Nin's symbol of destructive force. Only slowly did Nin come to valorize the dark side of her own nature, of human nature, and of the feminine – and to integrate it into her notion of creation. Wood concludes with a brief discussion of how Nin's evolving concept anticipates the theoretical issues in modern feminist thought.

Sophia Papachristou's "The Body in the Diary: On Anaïs Nin's First Erotic Writings" (1991) approaches the material in *Henry and June* as Nin's first conscious attempt at erotic writing. Papachristou suggests that ellipses and abruptness in Nin's erotic descriptions reflect the suspension of emotion. Other such generalizations about erotica, or female erotica, are drawn from Nin's example. A complementary study is Gislinde Seybert's "Between Love and Passion: Some Notes on the Physical in 'Henry & June' "(1991). Seybert argues that Nin's self-discovery through writing as well as her growth as a writer are tied to physical experiences "and with the unshackling of female sexuality from the bonds of prevailing conventions" (67). Seybert is particularly astute at pointing out how Nin negotiates the dichotomy between passion and love.

An attempt at tracing the sources of Nin's creativity, Kim Krizan's "Illusion and the Art of Survival" (1992) gathers evidence from the *Early Diary* as well as the *Diary*. Krizan finds a tension between accuracy and illusion that is at once limiting and liberating. Nin reveals herself, directly and indirectly, to be more comfortable in the world of illusion than the world of reality. Krizan locates the genesis of this orientation and of the *Diary* in childhood trauma although the response to this trauma colors the *Diary* throughout. Nin is always posturing as an optimist in her defensive escape from a core perception of reality that is essentially pessimistic. Having failed to seduce her father back into the family, she creates a seductive persona, "a dream of herself and her life" (28), to attract others.

It is difficult to know just where to place Elyse Lamm Pineau's fascinating "A Mirror of Her Own: Anaïs Nin's Autobiographical Performances" (1992). On the one hand, Pineau addresses a distinct phase in Nin's career: Nin as a special kind of celebrity performance artist. However, Pineau's analysis focuses on the way in which Nin's autobiographical text, the *Diary*, serves as script for Nin's public incarnations of her autobiographical heroine. Drawing upon the *Diary* as well as recordings of Nin's performances, Pineau observes how those performances fuse "her lived reality as the writer of the *Diary*, her inscribed reality as the *Diary* heroine 'Anaïs,' and her performance reality as a celebrity lecturer" (100). Nin's performances usually assumed that her spectators were familiar with the *Diary*, thus their imaginative impressions were confirmed, challenged, or reshaped by the dramatically realized Anaïs. Nin's performances were a logical final stage in her exemplary career of feminine self-construction. Having created a self in words, Nin came on stage to impersonate that self.

The most recent volume carved from Nin's diary, *Incest* (1992), has just become available to her critics. In his introduction, Rupert Pole promises future volumes in what is now called the "Journal of Love" series. From such materials, we can anticipate a continuing reassessment of Nin as diarist and as exemplary or representative figure. Fifteen years after Nin's death, her drama of gender continues.

Notes to Chapter 6

[1]In 1938, Miller announces in the issue of *The Phoenix* that reprinted "Un Être Étoilique" his plan to bring out the first volume of Nin's diary, as *Mon Journal*, in an edition of 250 copies to be printed in Belgium. This same issue includes a passage from Nin's "Winter of Artifice" titled "Orchestra." "Fragment from *Mon Journal*" appears in the Easter, 1940 issue. See also Miller's "Letter to William A. Bradley, Literary Agent," written in 1933 but not published until 1944, in which Miller scolds Bradley for suggesting cuts in the "Journal" in order to make it acceptable for publication.

[2]Hinz reviews volume 4 for two separate audiences. See " 'Excuse Me, It Was All a Dream': *The Diary of Anaïs Nin: 1944-1947*" and "Anaïs Nin" (both 1972). In "Anaïs Nin: A Reader and the Writer" (1975) Hinz reviews volume 5 of the *Diary* as well as the *Anaïs Nin Reader*, finding the editor's selections and arrangement amateurish and the project opportunistic.

[3]The first edition of Spencer's study treats the first six *Diary* volumes. The expanded edition also treats the seventh (and final) volume in that series as well as *Linotte*, the first installment of the four-volume *Early Diary of Anaïs Nin*.

[4]By comparison, attention to the *Diary* takes up about one sixth of Hinz's revised edition (four volumes treated), about one tenth of Knapp's book (six volumes treated), about one quarter of Spencer's expanded edition (seven volumes plus *Linotte* treated), about two fifths of Scholar's study (seven volumes plus two of the *Early Diary*).

[5]Scholar does recognize a strong appeal in "charming ingenuousness" (131) of the first two volumes of the posthumously published *Early Diary of Anaïs Nin*. She anticipates that the next two volumes will necessitate a new evaluation of the entire *Diary* enterprise.

[6]The particular works under discussion are Chodorow's *Psychoanalysis and the Psychology of Gender* and Rowbotham's *Women's Consciousness*.

[7]The three translations of German criticism in this issue of *Anaïs* are representative of Gunther Stuhlmann's tireless efforts to provide English readers with glimpses of Nin's international audience. These and the many other contributions from abroad found in the various issues certainly justify the ambitious subtitle "An International Journal."

[8] These same issues are addressed in my reference article, *"The Diary of Anaïs Nin"* (1989).

7: Conclusion

RESPONSES TO THE WRITING of Anaïs Nin range from the ecstatic praise of such strong partisans as Henry Miller, William Burford, Evelyn Hinz, Karl Shapiro, Sharon Spencer, and Bettina Knapp through the more tempered admiration of William Carlos Williams, Oliver Evans, Duane Schneider, Benjamin Franklin V, William Goyen, and Lynn Sukenick through the negative judgments of Diana Trilling, James Korges, Frank Baldanza, Joan Bobbitt, Estelle Jelinek, and Nancy Scholar. Prominent tastemakers like Edmund Wilson show excitement for the promise of Nin's earliest fiction, but much less enthusiasm for what follows. Soon after the publication of the first *Diary* volumes, the balance of attention to Nin's work begins to shift from the fiction to the *Diary*, but the fiction continues to stir interest and provoke appreciative response until the mid eighties.

In assessing Nin's various works of fiction, the major critics display intriguing patterns of agreement. By the very structure of their studies, Hinz and Spencer avoid making comparisons and contrasts among individual titles, though it is possible to assert – particularly in Spencer's work – that this is tantamount to accepting the grand orchestration of *Cities* as Nin's major achievement. Knapp clearly builds her discussion to argue that the early fictions are apprentice work on the road to the mature mastery of *Cities*. Evans, Franklin and Schneider, and Scholar all lean in the other direction. They hold up Nin's earlier and shorter fictions as her highest art. It is worth noting that this latter group is comprised of those who are less enthusiastic or at least more willing to find and address faults.

While Nin's critics have various judgments to make about the five *Cities* units, there is a consensus that *Heart* and *Seduction* are the most unified and coherent while *Spy* is the most experimentally ambitious. These are the judgments originally offered by Oliver Evans, who favors *Seduction* slightly, and they have held up quite well. For very different reasons, Korges and Demetrakopoulos single out *Heart*, while the popular *Spy* is often the focus of special studies (Balakian, Brians, Oliveira). Nonetheless, subsections of *Ladders* and *Children*, the first two novels, are recognized by Scholar and others to be among the most effective passages in Nin's writing. Some critics, Scholar included, treat *Cities* as the "continuous novel" it claims to be and thus have no reason for comparative judgments among the separate titles. Critics' explorations frequently attend to Nin's major characters, giving more attention to the construction of Lillian or Sabina or Djuna than to the novels in which they appear. In this regard, Hinz's book is the forerunner of a large body of later criticism.

Most of the major statements about Nin's fiction have attended to her characteristic modes of structure and style. On these matters, Hinz, Spencer, Knapp, and Balakian are most helpful. However, many charges about Nin's shortcomings as an artist have not been effectively countered. Explanations of image-motifs, symbolism, and allegory tell us what Nin does, but not how well, and the Nin student would be wise to explore the challenges presented by Baldanza, Korges, and others. Unfortunately, no collection presents a sampling of the arguments of Nin's detractors. The fact that there are few detailed stylistic analyses of individual Nin titles suggests that her work is not of a kind that rewards (or survives) such scrutiny.

Critics have noticed an irregular progression in Nin's fiction responsive to the Jungian dictum "proceed from the dream outward." The boundaries of the journey are marked by the almost total interiority of *House* on the one hand and the rich exteriority of *Seduction* along with the comic distancing of *Collages* on the other. While many observe that this movement parallels the pattern of psychic growth revealed in the shifting central figure (and in the subject of the *Diary* volumes), fewer would maintain that Nin's art is necessarily improved. A distinction between vision and artistic achievement must be maintained.

Nin's fiction was known to be diary-based long before the legendary diary itself was edited for an eager public. This knowledge has set the agenda for much of the fiction criticism, emphasizing its aspect as autobiographical writing (either as vivid distillation or abstract shadow) and thus raising the investigation of Nin herself (and her literary and personal relationships) to greater prominence than is perhaps healthy in literary inquiry. And, as Elizabeth Hardwick points out in her review of *Bell*, Nin's stories make reference to the diary (or a diary) in ways that ask the reader to take its significance on faith. Nin has admitted the problem of knowing which – diary or fiction – was her real work, and her critics have been similarly puzzled. Whatever the answer, the exploration of the (or "a") feminine self is the thematic starting point for most Nin criticism.

Since Nin's writings, from the beginning, have encouraged psychological interpretation, a central portion of the criticism responds to the challenge. In reviewing *This Hunger*, Diana Trilling accuses Nin of being a poor psychologist. Nonetheless, the Freudian readings by Henke; the Jungian approach of Demetrakopoulos; the Rankian responses by Potts, Spencer, and myself; and the Lacanian gambit of Richard-Allerdyce are only the most obvious reminders of how fruitfully Nin's literary constructs and concerns can be addressed by critics using psychoanalytic or psychological tools. Almost all extended discussions of Nin's work manifest an explicit or implicit psychoanalytic dimension. Critics like Balakian, Knapp, Kuntz, McEvilly, and Roof make skillful and appropriate use of psychoanalytic thought as part of their eclectic formulations. Kavaler-Adler reverses the process in her discussion of how Nin achieves a developmental form of mourning in her fiction.

Many of the psychoanalytic forays overlap with discussions that focus Nin's problematic status as a proto-feminist writer. The issue of Nin as a breakthrough "feminine" writer begins as early as 1942 with Williams's piece on *Winter*. Williams finds Nin at the threshold of a new feminine vision and style, but two years later Isaac Rosenfeld (writing about *Bell*) can discover none of the advance in feminine writing that he had (from others' comments) expected. This continuing debate includes the voices of Ellen Peck Killoh (who finds Nin's feminine vision of connectedness unachieved), Estelle C. Jelinek (for whom Nin's outsider and individualistic feminism is not politically correct), Julia Casterton (for whom Nin's erotica symtomize her discordant sounding among feminists), and Sharon Spencer (for whom Nin's example as a woman artist is one both of courage and achievement). Nancy Scholar separates the sources of Nin's appeal to women writers from her level of artistic achievement, while Dennis R. Miller considers Nin's erotica the successful feminine reformulation of a male genre. Almost all of those who write about Nin in a feminist context (Spencer is here the exception) fail to attend sufficiently to Nin's relationship with Otto Rank, a relationship through which many of Rank's own ideas were tested and sharpened toward his posthumously-published landmark essay "Feminine Psychology and Masculine Ideology" (1941).

Although Nin's work as a writer of fiction was all available years before the first book-length study of her work, selections from her voluminous diary continue to appear even since Scholar's study. During years spanned by the six books on Nin, *Diary* volumes were coming out on a regular basis, making discussions of this ongoing work tentative and skewing the proportions of attention to diary and fiction as each successive critical study has more *Diary* volumes to take into account (or ignore). Evans and Knapp treat the *Diary* only as sourcebook for the fiction. Hinz and Spencer consider its special generic and artistic properties, but neither seems ready to hold up the *Diary* as Nin's major achievement. Even though Franklin and Schneider make much less of a distinction between Nin's achievement in the two modes, and even as they claim that her fiction is undervalued, they seem to give the *Diary* the nod. Like Spencer, they view Nin's achievement less as a matter of genre mastery and more as sheer literary presence, power, and insight. "Her greatest value," they conclude, "is as a legitimate cicerone through the feminine psyche" (294). Scholar, who treats the *Diary* before the fiction and gives her discussion of each equal space, can state unequivocally that the *Diary* (to be judged as autobiography) outdistances all of Nin's other work as literature, and that the first two volumes are the finest (131).

Following the lead of Franklin and Schneider, many who write about the *Diary* are concerned with whom to credit for the shape of individual volumes. Critics would like to know more about Gunther Stuhlmann's role in preparing the first series, editorial credits for the *Early Diary*, and Rupert Pole's responsibility for *H&J*.

Most of the periodical criticism about Nin's writings in recent years is focused on the *Diary*, though there is occasional attention to the erotica. Critical writings about Nin's novels and stories have almost ceased to appear. Indeed, if one sets aside Spencer's anthology and Scholar's book, very little has been written about Nin's fiction since the end of the 1970s. In attending to Nin's achievement as diarist/autobiographer, critics have concerned themselves with recently fashionable issues: self-writing as a feminine mode, Nin's place in the women's movement, authenticity, and the new psychoanalytic criticism (exemplified by Lacan). The re-editing of Nin's diary that produced *H&J* and *Incest* is an ongoing enterprise, and more carvings from the "unexpurgated" diary will provide new glimpses of the woman and her art. These revelations will no doubt continue to draw attention away from Nin's achievement as a fiction writer and accelerate the tendency to view her, through her writings, as a case study.

Though at the present moment few Nin titles are readily available in bookstores, most are in print. Nin's position as a venturesome fiction writer of limited but noteworthy accomplishment seems secure, but less so than her status as biographer and mythmaker of and for herself as well as of and for a significant proportion of modern womanhood. The amount and range of attention that her writings have provoked establish her as an important, if not major voice in the literature of the central half of the twentieth century.

Bibliography

Works by Anaïs Nin: Principal Editions

D. H. Lawrence: An Unprofessional Study. Paris: Edward W. Titus, 1932. First American edition, Denver: Alan Swallow, 1964.

The House of Incest. Paris: Siana Editions, 1936. First American edition, New York: Gemor Press, 1947.

The Winter of Artifice. Paris: Obelisk Press, 1939; revised edition New York: Gemor Press, 1942; enlarged edition, Denver: Alan Swallow, 1961.

Under a Glass Bell. New York: Gemor Press, 1944; enlarged edition New York: E. P. Dutton, 1948.

This Hunger. New York: Gemor Press, 1945.

Ladders to Fire. New York: E. P. Dutton, 1946; shortened version, Denver: Alan Swallow, 1963.

Realism and Reality. Yonkers, N.Y.: Alicat Book Shop, 1946.

On Writing. Hanover, N.H.: Daniel Oliver Associates, 1947.

Children of the Albatross. New York: E. P. Dutton, 1947

The Four-Chambered Heart. New York: Duell, Sloan & Pierce, 1950.

A Spy in the House of Love. New York: British Book Centre, 1954.

Solar Barque. N.p.: n.p., 1958; expanded as *Seduction of the Minotaur*, Denver: Alan Swallow, 1961.

Cities of the Interior. N.p.: n.p., 1959; Denver: Alan Swallow, 1961; enlarged edition, Chicago: Swallow Press, 1974.

Collages. Denver: Alan Swallow, 1964.

The Diary of Anaïs Nin, 1931-1934. New York: Swallow Press and Harcourt, Brace & World, 1966. Vol. 1. [All seven volumes edited and with prefaces by Gunther Stuhlmann]

The Diary of Anaïs Nin, 1934-1939. New York: Harcourt, Brace & World, 1967. Vol. 2.

The Novel of the Future. New York: Macmillan, 1968.

The Diary of Anaïs Nin, 1939-1944. New York: Harcourt, Brace & World, 1969. Vol. 3.

The Diary of Anaïs Nin, 1944-1947. New York: Harcourt Brace Jovanovich, 1971. Vol. 4.

Anaïs Nin Reader. Edited and with a foreword by Philip K. Jason. Chicago: Swallow Press, 1973.

The Diary of Anaïs Nin, 1947-1955. New York: Harcourt Brace Jovanovich, 1974. Vol. 5.

A Woman Speaks: The Lectures, Seminars and Interviews of Anaïs Nin. Ed. Evelyn J. Hinz. Chicago: Swallow Press, 1975.

The Diary of Anaïs Nin, 1955-1966. New York: Harcourt Brace Jovanovich, 1976. Vol. 6.

In Favor of the Sensitive Man and Other Essays. New York: Harcourt Brace Jovanovich, 1976.

Delta of Venus: Erotica. New York: Harcourt Brace Jovanovich, 1977.

Waste of Timelessness and Other Early Stories. Weston, Conn.: Magic Circle Press, 1977.

Linotte. The Early Diary of Anaïs Nin, 1914-1920. Ed. John Ferrone New York: Harcourt Brace Jovanovich, 1978. *Early Diary*, vol. 1. [All volumes with prefaces by Joaquin Nin-Culmell]

Little Birds: Erotica. New York: Harcourt Brace Jovanovich, 1979.

The Diary of Anaïs Nin, 1966-1974. New York: Harcourt Brace Jovanovich, 1980. Vol. 7.

The Early Diary of Anaïs Nin, 1920-1923. New York: Harcourt Brace Jovanovich, 1982. *Early Diary*, vol. 2. [This and succeeding volumes edited by Rupert Pole]

The Early Diary of Anaïs Nin, 1923-1927. San Diego: Harcourt Brace Jovanovich, 1983. *Early Diary*, vol. 3.

The Early Diary of Anaïs Nin, 1927-1931. San Diego: Harcourt Brace Jovanovich, 1985. *Early Diary*, vol. 4.

The White Blackbird and Other Writings. Santa Barbara: Capra Press, 1985.

Henry and June: From the Unexpurgated Diary of Anaïs Nin. Edited and with a preface by Rupert Pole. San Diego: Harcourt Brace Jovanovich, 1986.

A Literate Passion: Letters of Anaïs Nin and Henry Miller. Edited and with an introduction by Gunther Stuhlmann. San Diego: Harcourt Brace Jovanovich, 1987.

Incest: From "A Journal of Love," The Unexpurgated Diary of Anaïs Nin, 1932-1934. Introduction by Rupert Pole and Biographical Notes by Gunther Stuhlmann. San Diego: Harcourt Brace Jovanovich, 1992.

Critical Works

Alberti, Frank S. "Anaïs Nin, Reader of Proust: The Creative Affinities." *Under the Sign of Pisces: Anaïs Nin and Her Circle* 10.2 (Spring 1979): 3-12.

Andersen, Margret. "Critical Approaches to Anaïs Nin." *Canadian Review of American Studies* 10.2 (Fall 1979): 255-65.

Balakian, Anna. "Anaïs Nin and Feminism." Spencer 23-33. Rpt. as "A Tale of Two People" in *Anaïs: An International Journal* 6 (1988): 58-66.

_____. "The Poetic Reality of Anaïs Nin." Introduction to *Anaïs Nin Reader*. Ed. Philip K. Jason. Chicago: Swallow Press, 1973. 11-30. Rpt. in Harms's *Celebration with Anaïs Nin* and in Zaller 113-31.

_____. " '. . . and the pursuit of happiness': *The Scarlet Letter* and *A Spy in the House of Love*." Hinz 163-70.

_____. Rev. of *Anaïs Nin* by Oliver Evans. *American Literature* 41.1 (Mar. 1969): 130-33.

Baldanza, Frank. "Anaïs Nin." *Minnesota Review* 2 (Winter 1962): 263-71.

Barnes, Daniel. "Nin and Traditional Erotica." *Seahorse: The Anaïs Nin/Henry Miller Journal* 1.1 (1982): 1-5.
Benstock, Benjamin. "The Present Recaptured: D. H. Lawrence and Others." *Southern Review* NS 4 (July 1968): 802-16. Rev. of *Diary* 1.

Benstock, Shari. *Women of the Left Bank: Paris, 1900-1940.* Austin: University of Texas Press, 1986.

Bloom, Lynn Z., and Orlee Holder. "Anaïs Nin's *Diary* in Context." Hinz 191-202. Rpt. in *Women's Autobiography: Essays in Criticism.* Ed. Estelle C. Jelinek. Bloomington: Indiana University Press, 1980. 206-20.

Bobbitt, Joan. "Truth and Artistry in the *Diary of Anaïs Nin.*" *Journal of Modern Literature* 9.2 (May 1982): 267-76.

Bradbury, Malcolm. "Aesthetic Decadence." *Manchester Guardian* 12 Sept. 1968: 14. On *Bell.*

_____. "New Novels." *Punch* 21 June 1961: 953-54. On *Seduction.*

Bradford, Jean. "The Self: A Mosaic, A Loving Perspective on the Diaries of Anaïs Nin." *Journal of the Otto Rank Association* 12.1 (Summer 1977): 14-25.

Brandon, Dolores. "Anaïs Nin: Sister to the Creators of Modern Dance." Spencer 101-24.

Brians, Paul. "Sexuality and the Opposite Sex: Variations on a Theme by Théophile Gautier and Anaïs Nin." *Essays in Literature* 4 (Spring 1977): 122-37.

"Briefly Noted – Fiction." *New Yorker* 12 Dec. 1964: 244. On *Collages.*

Broderick, Catherine. "Anaïs Nin's *Diary* and the Japanese Literary Diary Tradition." Hinz 177-89.

_____. "The Song of the Womanly Soul: Mask and Revelation in Japanese Literature and in the Fiction of Anaïs Nin." Spencer 176-91.

Broderick, Catherine, with Masako Karatani. "The Reception of Anaïs Nin in Japan." *Under the Sign of Pisces: Anaïs Nin and Her Circle* 5.1 (Winter 1974): 5-11.

Brodin, Pierre. "Anaïs Nin." *Vingt-Cinq Américains: Littérature et Littératurs Américains Des Années 1960.* Paris: Nouvelles Editions Debresse, 1969.

Burford, William. "The Art of Anaïs Nin." In *On Writing*, by Anaïs Nin. Hanover, N.H.: Daniel Oliver Associates, 1947. 5-14. Pamphlet rpt. Yonkers, N.Y.: Alicat Bookshop, 1947, as number 11 in the Outcast Chapbook series. Essay rpt. in *Anaïs: An International Journal* 8 (1990): 40-44. (Text cited from this last edition.)

Carruth, Hayden. *"The Four-Chambered Heart." Providence Sunday Journal* 29 Jan. 1950: 10.

Casey, Florence. "A Bird Does not Need to Study Aviation." *Christian Science Monitor* 14 Jan. 1969, C: 1. On *Novel.*

Célérier, Patricia-Pia. "The Vision of Dr. Allendy: Psychoanalysis and the Quest for an Independent Identity." *Anaïs: An International Journal* 7 (1989): 78-94.

Centing, Richard R. "Emotional Algebra: The Symbolic Level of *The Diary of Anaïs Nin, 1944-1947.*" Zaller 169-76.

Chase, Gilbert Culmell. "From 'Kew' to Paris: A Personal Memoir." *Anaïs: An International Journal* 1 (1983): 60-62.

Chase, Kathleen. "Anaïs Nin and Music: Jazz." *Under the Sign of Pisces: Anaïs Nin and Her Circle* 11.1 (Winter 1980): 15-22.

_____. "Anaïs Nin – Rumour and Reality: A Memoir by Kathleen Chase." *Under the Sign of Pisces: Anaïs Nin and Her Circle* 6.4 (Fall 1975): 1-8.

_____. "Being 'Family' in France, 1930-1934." *Anaïs: An International Journal* 1 (1983): 63-66.

_____. *"Cities of the Interior*, by Anaïs Nin." *Two Cities: La Revue Bilingue de Paris* 15 May 1960: 100-03. Unsigned.

Clark, Orville. "Anaïs Nin: Studies in the New Erotology." Zaller 101-11.

Cole, Barry. "Soothsayers." *The Spectator*. 13 Sept. 1968. On *Bell*.

"Collages by Anaïs Nin." *Los Angeles Free Press* 26 Nov. 1964: 8.

Cushman, Keith. "The View from *Under a Glass Bell*." Hinz 110-19.

Cutting, Rose Marie. *Anaïs Nin: A Reference Guide*. Boston: G. K. Hall, 1978.

"D. H. Lawrence in Retrospect." *Times Literary Supplement* 5 May 1932: 327.

Davis, Robert Gorham. "Anaïs Nin's Children of Light and Movement." *New York Times Book Review* 23 Nov. 1947: 36. On *Children*.

_____. "The Fantastic World of Anaïs Nin." *New York Times Book Review* 28 Mar. 1948: 24. On *Bell*.

Dearborn, Mary V. *The Happiest Man Alive: A Biography of Henry Miller*. New York: Simon & Schuster, 1991.

Deduck, Patricia A. *Realism, Reality, and the Fictional Theory of Alain Robbe-Grillet and Anaïs Nin*. Washington, D.C.: University Press of America, 1982.

Demetrakopoulos, Stephanie A. "Anaïs Nin and the Feminine Quest for Consciousness: The Quelling of the Devouring Mother and the Ascension of the Sophia." *Women, Literature, Criticism*. Ed. Harry R. Garvin and Catherine F. Smith. Lewisburg, Penn.: Bucknell University Press, 1978. Simultaneously a special issue of *Bucknell Review* 24.1 (Spring 1978): 119-36.

_____. "Archetypal Constellations of Feminine Consciousness in Nin's First *Diary*." Hinz 121-37.

Dennison, Sally. "Anaïs Nin: The Book as a Work of Art." *Alternative Literary Publishing: Five Modern Histories*. Iowa City: University of Iowa Press, 1984. 119-55.

Dick, Bernard F. "Anaïs Nin and Gore Vidal: A Study in Literary Incompatibility." Hinz 153-62.

Durrell, Lawrence. Preface to *Children of the Albatross*. London: Peter Owen, 1959. 9-10. Rpt. in Zaller 2.

Edel, Leon. "Life Without Father." *Saturday Review* 7 May 1966: 91. On *Diary* 1.

Ekberg, Kent. "The Importance of *Under a Glass Bell.*" *Under the Sign of Pisces: Anaïs Nin and Her Circle* 8.2 (Spring 1977): 4-18.

_____. *"Waste of Timelessness and Other Early Stories* by Anaïs Nin." *Under the Sign of Pisces: Anaïs Nin and Her Circle* 8.3 (Summer 1977): 12-17.

Ellmann, Mary. *Thinking About Women.* New York: Harcourt Brace Jovanovich, 1968.

Evans, Oliver. *Anaïs Nin.* Carbondale: Southern Illinois University Press, 1968.

_____. "Anaïs Nin and the Discovery of Inner Space." *Prairie Schooner* 36 (Fall 1962): 217-31.

Faas, Ekbert. " 'The Barbaric Friendship with Robert': A Biographical Palimpsest." Hinz 141-52.

_____. *Young Robert Duncan: Portrait of the Poet As Homosexual in Society.* Santa Barbara: Black Sparrow Press, 1983.

Fancher, Edwin. "Anaïs Nin: Avant-Gardist with a Loyal Underground." *Village Voice* 27 May 1959: 4-5.

Fanchette, Jean. "Notes pour une Préface." *Two Cities: La Revue Bilingue de Paris* 15 Apr. 1959: 56-60.

Ferguson, Robert. *Henry Miller: A Life.* New York: W. W. Norton, 1991.

Ferrone, John. "The Making of *Delta of Venus.*" Spencer 35-43.

Ford, Hugh. *Published in Paris: American and British Writers, Printers, and Publishers in Paris, 1920-1939.* New York: Macmillan, 1975.

Fowlie, Wallace. Rev. of *Anaïs Nin Reader. New York Times Book Review* 9 Sept. 1973: 26-27.

Franklin, Benjamin, V. "AN and the Rare Book Trade." *Under the Sign of Pisces: Anaïs Nin and Her Circle* 3.1 (Winter 1972): 11-16.

_____. "AN's Recordings, Editorship of Periodicals, and Films." *Under the Sign of Pisces: Anaïs Nin and Her Circle* 2.4 (Fall 1971): 7-10.

_____. "Anaïs Nin." *American Writers in Paris, 1920-1929. Dictionary of Literary Biography 4.* Ed. Karen Lane Rood. Detroit: Gale Research, 1980.

_____. "Anaïs Nin: A Bibliographical Essay." Zaller 25-33.

_____. *Anaïs Nin: A Bibliography.* Kent, Ohio: The Kent State University Press, 1973.

_____. "The Textual Evolution of the First Section of 'Houseboat.' " Hinz 95-106.

Franklin, Benjamin, V, and Duane Schneider. *Anaïs Nin: An Introduction.* Athens: Ohio University Press, 1979.

Friedman, Ellen G. "Anaïs Nin." *Modern American Women Writers.* Ed. Lea Baechler, A. Walton Litz, and Elaine Showalter. New York: Charles Scribner's Sons, 1991. 339-51.

_____. "Escaping from the House of Incest: On Anaïs Nin's Efforts to Overcome Patriarchal Constraints." *Anaïs: An International Journal* 10 (1992): 39-45.

Friedman, Melvin J. "André Malraux and Anaïs Nin." *Contemporary Literature* 11.1 (Winter 1970): 104-13. Rev. of Evans.

Friedman, Susan Stanford. "Women's Autobiographical Selves: Theory and Practice." In *The Private Self: Theory and Practice of Women's Autobiographical Writings.* Ed. Shari Benstock. Chapel Hill: University of North Carolina Press, 1988. 34-62.

Fuller, John. "In the Truck." *New Statesman* 1 May 1964: 688. On *Collages.*

Fülop-Miller, René. "Freudian Noah's Ark." *New York Times* 29 Jan. 1950: 4. On *Heart.*

Garoffolo, Vincent. Rev.of *Under the Glass Bell and Other Stories. New Mexico Quarterly Review* 18 (Summer 1948): 247-49.

Geismar, Maxwell. "Anaïs Nin: An Imprecise Spy in the House of Love." *Los Angeles Times* 13 May 1979, sec. 5: 3.

_____. "Temperament vs. Conscience." *The Nation* 24 July 1954: 75-76. On *Spy*.

Gilbert, Sandra M. "Feminism and D. H. Lawrence." *Anaïs: An International Journal* 9 (1991): 92-100.

Gilbert, Stuart. "Foreword to *House of Incest*." Zaller 1. A portion appears in *Dairy* 2, 146-47.

_____. "Passion in Parenthesis." *Reading and Collecting* 1.12 (Nov. 1937): 23. On *House*.

Gottlieb, Elaine S. "New Fiction of America." New York *Herald Tribune Books* 8 Nov. 1942: 14. On *Winter*.

Goyen, William. "Bits and Images of Life." *New York Times Book Review* 29 Nov. 1964: 5, 24. On *Collages*.

_____. "Portrait of the Artist as Diarist." *New York Times Book Review* 14 Apr. 1974: 4. On *Diary* 5.

Graham, Kenneth. "Ruined Raj." *The Listener* 5 Sept. 1968: 313. On *Bell*.

Griffin, Barbara J. "Two Experimental Writers: Djuna Barnes and Anaïs Nin." *American Women Writers: Bibliographical Essays*. Ed. Maurice Duke, Jackson R. Bryer, and M. Thomas Inge. Westport, Conn.: Greenwood Press, 1983. 144-66.

Griffith, Paul. "The 'Jewels' of Anaïs Nin." *Journal of the Otto Rank Association* 5.2 (Dec. 1970): 82-89.

Hahn, Emily. "*Winter of Artifice*." *T'ien Hsia Monthly* Nov. 1939: 435-38.

Haller, Robert A. "Anaïs Nin and Film: Open Questions." Spencer 135-38.

Hardwick, Elizabeth. "Fiction Chronicle." *Partisan Review* 15 (June 1948): 705-11. On *Bell*.

Harms, Valerie. "Anaïs Nin, Witch of Words." *Maria Montessori, Anaïs Nin, Frances Steloff: Stars in My Sky*. Riverside, Conn.: Magic Circle Press, 1975. 82-118.

_____, ed. *Celebration with Anaïs Nin*. Riverside, Conn.: Magic Circle Press, 1973.

_____. "The Dream Is the Key – The Drafts That Became *House of Incest*." *Anaïs: An International Journal* 5 (1987): 102-10.

_____. "Interaction and Cross-Fertilization: Miller and Nin." *Anaïs: An International Journal* 4 (1986): 109-15.

Hart, William. "Analysis of the Antagonisms Inherent in the Human Struggle." *Houston Post* 16 Nov. 1947, sec. 4: 21. On *Children*.

Hauser, Marianne. "Anaïs Nin: Myth and Reality." *Studies in the Twentieth Century* 2 (Fall 1968): 45-50.

_____. "Thoughts on *The Diary of Anaïs Nin*." *Journal of the Otto Rank Association* 5.1 (June 1970): 61-67.

Henke, Suzette A. "Anaïs Nin: Bread and the Wafer." *Under the Sign of Pisces: Anaïs Nin and Her Circle* 7.2 (Spring 1976): 7-17.

_____. "Anaïs Nin: A Freudian Perspective." *Under the Sign of Pisces: Anaïs Nin and Her Circle* 11.1 (Winter 1980): 6-14.

_____. "Lillian Beye's Labyrinth: A Freudian Exploration of *Cities of the Interior*." *Anaïs: An International Journal* 2 (1984): 113-26.

"Herself Surprised." *Times Literary Supplement* 24 July 1969: 829. On *Novel*.

Hicks, Granville. Rev. of *The Novel of the Future*. *Saturday Review* 25 Jan. 1969: 25-26.

Hinz, Evelyn J. "Anaïs Nin." *Contemporary Literature* 13.2 (Spring 1972): 255-257. On *Diary* 4.

_____. "Anaïs Nin: A Reader and the Writer." *The Canadian Review of American Studies* 6.1 (Spring 1975): 116-27.

_____. "The Creative Critic." Harms 57-65.

_____. " 'Excuse Me, It Was All a Dream': *The Diary of Anaïs Nin, 1944-1947*." *Journal of the Otto Rank Association* 7.2 (Dec. 1972): 21-36.

_____. *The Mirror and the Lamp: Realism and Reality in the Writings of Anaïs Nin*. [Columbus]: Ohio State University Libraries, 1971. Revised ed. New York: Harcourt Brace Jovanovich, 1973.

_____. "Recent Nin Criticism: Who's on First?" *Canadian Review of American Studies* 13.3 (Winter 1982): 373-88.

_____, ed. *The World of Anaïs Nin: Critical and Cultural Perspectives*. Winnipeg: University of Manitoba Press, 1978. Simultaneously a special issue of *Mosaic* 11.2 (Winter 1978).

Hodgart, Patricia. "Fire of Exile." *The Spectator* 26 May 1961: 771. On *Seduction*.

"Hothouse Crusader." *Times Literary Supplement* 29 Jan. 1971: 113. On *Spy*.

Hoy, Nancy Jo. "The Poetry of Experience." *Anaïs: An International Journal* 4 (1986): 52-66.

Hugo, Ian. "The Making of *Bells of Atlantis*." Hinz 77-80.

Jason, Philip K. "Anaïs Nin." *Research Guide to Biography and Criticism*. Ed. Walton Beachum. Washington, D.C.: Research Publishing, 1985.

_____. "A Delicate Battle Cry – Anaïs Nin's Pamphlets of the 1940s." *Anaïs: An International Journal* 8 (1990): 30-34.

_____. "*The Diary of Anaïs Nin*." *Masterplots II: Nonfiction Series*. Pasadena: Salem Press, 1989.

_____. "Doubles/Don Juans: Anaïs Nin and Otto Rank." Hinz 81-94.

_____. "Dropping Another Veil." *Anaïs: An International Journal* 6 (1988): 27-32. On *H&J*.

_____. Foreword. *Anaïs Nin Reader*. Ed. Philip K. Jason. Chicago: Swallow Press, 1973. 1-8. Rpt. New York: Avon Books, 1974. 1-8.

_____. "The Future of Nin Criticism, A Review." *Journal of the Otto Rank Association* 7.1 (June 1972): 82-90. On Hinz.

_____. "The Gemor Press." *Anaïs: An International Journal* 2 (1984): 24-39.

_____. "Oscar Baradinsky's 'Outcasts': Henry Miller, Anaïs Nin, Maya Deren and The Alicat Book Shop Press." *Anaïs: An International Journal* 3 (1985): 109-16.

_____. "The Princess and the Frog: Anaïs Nin and Otto Rank." Spencer 13-22.

_____. Rev. of *Collage of Dreams* by Sharon Spencer. *Style* 12.3 (Summer 1978): 311.

_____. "Teaching *A Spy in the House of Love.*" *Under the Sign of Pisces: Anaïs Nin and Her Circle* 2.3 (Summer 1971): 7-15.

_____. "Warring Against Her Partisans." *Anaïs: An International Journal* 4 (1986): 123-126. On Scholar.

Jelinek, Estelle C. "Anaïs Nin: A Critical Evaluation." In *Feminist Criticism.* Ed. Cheryl L. Brown and Karen Olson. Metuchen, N.J.: Scarecrow Press, 1978. 312-23.

Jennings, Elizabeth. "New Novels." *Listener* 7 May 1964: 769. On *Collages.*

John-Steiner, Vera. "From Life to Diary to Art in the Work of Anaïs Nin." *Creative People at Work: Twelve Cognitive Case Studies.* Ed. Doris B. Wallace and Howard E. Gruber. New York: Oxford University Press, 1989. 210-25.

Kamboureli, Smaro. "Discourse and Intercourse, Design and Desire in the Erotica of Anaïs Nin." *Journal of Modern Literature* 11.1 (March 1984): 143-58.

Karsten, Julie A. "Self-Realization and Intimacy: The Influence of D. H. Lawrence on Anaïs Nin." *Anaïs: An International Journal* 4 (1986): 36-42.

Kavaler-Adler. Susan. "Anaïs Nin and the Developmental Use of the Creative Process." *Psychoanalytic Review* 79.1 (Spring 1992): 73-88.

Keith, Kay. *"Ladders to Fire."* San Francisco Chronicle 8 Dec. 1946, "This World" sec.: 11.

Kennedy, J. Gerald. "Place, Self, and Writing." *The Southern Review* 26.3 (Summer 1990): 496-516. Section on Nin 505-11.

Killoh, Ellen Peck. "The Woman Writer and the Element of Destruction." *College English* 34.1 (Oct. 1972): 31-38.

Kingery, Robert E. "New Books Appraised – Fiction." *Library Journal* 1 Jan. 1948: 40. On *Bell*.

Kirsch, Robert. "Anaïs Nin's Literary Labyrinth." *Los Angeles Times* 27 Apr. 1973, sec. 4: 14. On *Reader*.

Knapp, Bettina L. *Anaïs Nin*. New York: Ungar, 1978. (Some of the material from Knapp's chapter on *House* also appears as "Anaïs/Artaud – Alchemy" in Hinz 66-74.

_____. "The Diary as Art: Anaïs Nin, Thornton Wilder, Edmund Wilson." *World Literature Today* 61.2 (Spring 1987): 223-30.

_____. *"The Novel of the Future."* *The Village Voice* 10 Apr. 1969: 6-7.

_____. " 'To Reach Out Further Mystically...' Anaïs Nin." *Research Studies* 47.3 (Sept. 1979): 165-80. Rpt. in Spencer 65-85.

Korges, James. "Curiosities: Nin and Miller, Hemingway and Seager." *Critique: Studies in Modern Fiction* 7.3 (Spring-Summer 1965): 66-81.

Kraft, Barbara. "Lux Aeterna Anaïs: A Memoir." *Seahorse: The Anaïs Nin/Henry Miller Journal* 2.2, 2.3, and 2.4 (1983): 1-5, 1-7, and 6-16.

Krizan, Kim. "Illusion and the Art of Survival." *Anaïs: An International Journal* 10 (1992): 18-28.

Kubasak, Sharon. "Doing the Limbo with Woolf and Nin: On Writer's Block." *Centennial Review* 32.4 (Fall 1988): 372-87.

Kuntz, Paul Grimley. "Anaïs Nin's 'Quest for Order.' " Hinz 203-212.

_____. "Art as Public Dream: The Practice and Theory of Anaïs Nin." *Journal of Aesthetics and Art Criticism* 32 (Summer 1974): 525-37. Rpt. in Zaller 77-99.

Lang, Violet R. Rev. of *Under a Glass Bell* and *Children of the Albatross*. *Chicago Review* 2.4 (Spring 1948): 162-63.

Lawlor, Patricia. "Beyond Gender and Genre: Writing the Labyrinth of the Selves." *Anaïs: An International Journal* 7 (1989): 23-31.

Legman, Gershon. "The Erotica of Henry Miller and Anaïs Nin." *Under the Sign of Pisces: Anaïs Nin and Her Circle* 12.3-4 (Summer/Fall 1981):

9-18.

_____. Introduction. *The Private Case: An Annotated Bibliography of the Private Case Erotica Ellection in the British Library*. Comp. Patrick J. Kearney. London: Jay Landesman Ltd., 1981. 11-59.

Lieberman, E. James. *Acts of Will: The Life and Works of Otto Rank*. New York: Free Press, 1985.

Lyons, Herbert. "Surrealist Soap Opera." *New York Times Book Review* 20 Oct. 1946: 16. On *Ladders*.

Lytle, Andrew. "Impressionism, the Ego, and the First Person." *Daedalus* 92 (Spring 1963): 281-296. On *Cities*, p. 285.

McEvilly, Wayne. "The Two Faces of Death in Anaïs Nin's *Seduction of the Minotaur*." *New Mexico Quarterly* 38 (Winter-Spring 1969): 179-192. Rpt. as "Afterword" to the fourth and later Swallow printings of the novel and in Zaller 51-64.

_____. "Portrait of Anaïs Nin as a Bodhisattva: Reflections on the *Diary, 1934-39*." *Studies in the Twentieth Century* 2 (Fall 1968): 51-60.

_____. "The Bread of Tradition: Reflections on the Diary of Anaïs Nin." *Prairie Schooner* 45 (Summer 1971): 161-67.

_____. "A Map of Music – Strange Dimensions of Politics and War." Spencer 126-33.

McLaughlin, Richard. "Shadow Dance." *Saturday Review* 20 Dec. 1947: 16-17. On *Children*.

MacNiven, Ian S. "Criticism and Personality: Lawrence Durrell – Anaïs Nin." *Anaïs: An International Journal* 2 (1984): 95-100.

_____. "A Room in the House of Art: The Friendship of Anaïs Nin and Lawrence Durrell." Hinz 37-58.

Marcinczyk, Reese. "A Checklist of the Writings of Anaïs Nin, 1973-1976." *Under the Sign of Pisces: Anaïs Nin and Her Circle* 8.1 (Winter 1977): 2-14.

Margoshes, Adam. *"Seduction of the Minotaur." Village Voice* 10 May 1962: 5-6.

Martin, Jay. *Always Merry and Bright: The Life of Henry Miller.* Santa Barbara: Capra Press, 1978.

Martin, Jex, Jr. "Modern Version of Old Fable: Woman Loses Femininity When She Enters Man's World." *Chicago Sun Book Week* 17 Nov. 1946: 14. On *Ladders.*

Mathieu, Bertrand. "On the Trail of Euridice." *Anaïs: An International Journal* 10 (1992): 63-76.

Merchant, Hoshang. "Out of and into the Labyrinth: Approaching the Aesthetics of Anaïs Nin." *Anaïs: An International Journal* 8 (1990): 51-59.

Metzger, Deena. "The *Diary*: The Ceremony of Knowing." Zaller 133-43.

Miller, Dennis R. *"Delta of Venus*: Sex from Female Perspectives." *Seahorse: The Anaïs Nin/Henry Miller Journal* 1.4 (1982): 6-11.

_____. "Glimpsing a Goddess: Some Thoughts on the Final *Diary*." *Anaïs: An International Journal* 3 (1985): 102-08.

Miller, Henry. "Letter to William A. Bradley, Literary Agent." *Sunday After the War.* Norfolk, Conn.: New Directions, 1944. 276-84.

_____. "On *House of Incest*: A 'Foreword' and a 'Review.' " *Anaïs: An International Journal* 5 (1987): 111-14.

_____. "Scenario." *The Cosmological Eye.* Norfolk, Conn.: New Directions, 1939. 75-106.

_____. "To Anaïs Nin Regarding One of Her Books." *Circle* 1.2 (1944): n. pag. Rpt. in *Sunday After the War.* Norfolk, Conn.: New Directions, 1944. 284-97.

_____. "Un Être Étoilique." *The Criterion* 17 (Oct. 1937): 35-52. Rpt. in *The Phoenix* 1 (June-Aug. 1938): 67-94. First collected in *The Cosmological Eye.* Norfolk, Conn.: New Directions, 1939, 269-91. Also in Zaller 5-23 (page references to this edition).

Miller, Margaret. "Diary-Keeping and the Young Wife." *Anais: An International Journal* 3 (1985): 39-44.

_____. "Seduction and Subversion in *The Diary of Anaïs Nin*." *Anaïs: An International Journal* 1 (1983): 86-90.

Millett, Kate. "Anaïs – A Mother to Us All: The Birth of the Artist as Woman." *Anaïs: An International Journal* 9 (1991): 3-8.

Molyneux, Maxine, and Julia Casterton. "Looking Again at Anaïs Nin." *Minnesota Review* 18 (Spring 1982): 86-101.

Moore, Harry T. Introduction. *D. H. Lawrence: An Unprofessional Study*, by Anaïs Nin. Denver: Alan Swallow, 1964. 7-14.

Mudrick, Marvin. "Humanity is the Principle." *Hudson Review* 7.4 (Winter 1955): 610-19. On *Spy*.

Niemeyer, Doris. "How to Be a Woman and/or an Artist: The Diary as an Instrument of Self-Therapy." Trans. Gunther Stuhlmann. *Anaïs: An International Journal* 6 (1988): 67-74.

"Nin, Anaïs." *Current Biography* (Feb. 1944): 493-95. Rpt. in Nin's *Realism and Reality*.

Nin, Anaïs, and Henry Miller. *A Literate Passion: Letters of Anaïs Nin and Henry Miller, 1932-1953*. Ed. Gunther Stuhlmann. San Diego: Harcourt Brace Jovanovich, 1987.

Norse, Harold. *Memoirs of a Bastard Angel*. New York: William Morrow, 1989.

"Not to Need, but To Be Needed." *Times Literary Supplement* 12 May 1972: 552. On *Diary* 4.

Oliveira, Ubiratan Paiva de. "*A Spy in the House of Love*: An Introduction to Anaïs Nin." *Ilha do Desterro* 14.2 (1985): 71-81.

Paine, Sylvia. *Beckett, Nabokov, Nin: Motives and Modernism*. Port Washington, N.Y.: Kennikat Press, 1981.

Papachristou, Sophia. "The Body in the Diary: On Anaïs Nin's First Erotic Writings." *Anaïs: An International Journal* 9 (1991): 58-66.

Pétrequin, Marie-Line. "The Magic Spell of June Miller: On the Literary Creation of Female Identity in Anaïs Nin's *Diary*." Trans. Gunther Stuhlmann. *Anaïs: An International Journal* 6 (1988): 43-57.

Perlès, Alfred. "Fathers, Daughters and Lovers." *Purpose* 12.1 (Jan.-Mar. 1940): 45-48. On *Winter*.

Pineau, Elyse Lamm. "A Mirror of Her Own: Anaïs Nin's Autobiographical Performances." *Text and Performance Quarterly* 12.1 (Apr. 1992): 98-112.

Potts, Margaret Lee. "The Genesis and Evolution of the Creative Personality: A Rankian Analysis of *The Diary of Anaïs Nin*." *Journal of the Otto Rank Association* 9.2 (Winter 1974-75): 1-37.

"Private View." *Times Literary Supplement* 16 Mar. 1962: 186. On *Lawrence*.

Rainer, Tristine. "Anaïs Nin's *Diary I*: The Birth of the Young Woman as an Artist." Zaller 161-68.

Rank, Otto. "Preface to *House of Incest*." *Anaïs: An International Journal* 3 (1985): 49-54. First published in *Journal of the Otto Rank Association* 7.2 (Dec. 1972): 68-74.

―――. "Reflections on the Diary of a Child." *Journal of the Otto Rank Association* 7.2 (Dec. 1972): 61-67.

―――. "Feminine Psychology and Masculine Ideology." *Beyond Psychology*. Philadelphia: E. Hauser, 1941. Rpt. New York: Dover, 1958. 235-70.

Rev. of *Under a Glass Bell and Other Stories*. New York *Herald Tribune Weekly Book Review* 21 Nov. 1948: 33.

Richard-Allerdyce, Diane. "Anaïs Nin's Mothering Metaphor: Toward a Lacanian Theory of Feminine Creativity." *Compromise Formations: Current Directions in Psychoanalytic Criticism*. Ed. Vera J. Camden. Kent, Ohio: Kent State University Press, 1989.

Roditi, Edouard. "On Proust and Pierre-Quint." *Anaïs: An International Journal* 7 (1989): 95-101.

Rolo, Charles. "The Life of the Heart." *Atlantic* (Feb. 1950): 86-87. On *Heart*.

―――. "Potpourri." *Atlantic* (Aug. 1954): 86. On *Spy*.

Roof, Judith. "The Erotic Travelogue: The Scopophilic Pleasure of Race vs. Gender." *Arizona Quarterly* 47.4 (Winter 1991): 119-35.

Root, Waverley Lewis. "The Femininity of D. H. Lawrence Emphasized by Woman Writer." *Chicago Daily Tribune* (European edition) 28 Mar. 1932: 2. Rpt. as "Literary Sexism in Action" in *Anaïs: An International Journal* 6 (1988): 75-76.

Rosenblatt, Jon. "Anaïs Nin's Allegories." *Under the Sign of Pisces: Anaïs Nin and Her Circle* 10.4 (Fall 1979): 8-12.

Rosenfeld, Isaac. "The Eternal Feminine." *New Republic* 17 Apr. 1944: 541. On *Bell*.

_____. "Psychoanalysis as Literature." *New Republic* 17 Dec. 1945: 844-45. On *This Hunger*.

Rosenfeld, Paul. "Refinements on a Journal: *Winter of Artifice* by Anaïs Nin." *The Nation* 26 Sept. 1942): 276-77.

Sagulo, Veronica Park. "The Italian Response: How the Critics Dealt with Anaïs Nin's Work." *Anaïs: An International Journal* 6 (1988): 111-17.

Salber, Linde. "Two Lives – One Experiment: Lou Andreas-Salomé and Anaïs Nin." Trans. Gunther Stuhlmann. *Anaïs: An International Journal* 9 (1991): 78-91.

Sayre, Gary. "*House of Incest*: Two Interpretations." Spencer 45-58.

Schneider, Duane. "Anaïs Nin in the *Diary*: The Creation and Development of a Persona." Hinz 9-19.

_____. "The Art of Anaïs Nin." *Southern Review* 6.2 ns (Apr. 1970): 506-514. Rpt. in Zaller 43-50.

_____. "The Duane Schneider Press and Anaïs Nin." *Under the Sign of Pisces: Anaïs Nin and Her Circle* 4.1 (Winter 1973): 5-9.

Scholar, Nancy. *Anaïs Nin*. Boston: Twayne, 1984.

_____. "Anaïs Nin Under a Glass Bell." *Michigan Quarterly Review* 20.3 (Summer 1981): 308-12.

_____. "Anaïs Nin's *House of Incest* and Ingmar Bergman's *Persona*: Two Variations on a Theme." *Literature/Film Quarterly* 7.1 (1979): 47-59. Rpt. in Spencer.

_____. "A Checklist of Nin Materials at Northwestern University Library." *Under the Sign of Pisces: Anaïs Nin and Her Circle* 3.2 (Spring 1972): 3-11. (As Nancy Scholar Zee).

Schwichtenberg, Cathy. "Erotica: The Semey Side of Semiotics." *SubStance* 32 (1981): 26-38.

Secrest, Meryle. "Economics and the Need for Revenge." *Anaïs: An International Journal* 6 (1988): 33-35.

Seybert, Gislinde. "Between Love and Passion: Some Notes on the Physical in 'Henry & June.' " Trans. Gunther Stuhlmann. *Anaïs: An International Journal* 9 (1991): 67-74.

Shapiro, Karl. "The Charmed Circle of Anaïs Nin." *Book Week* 1 May 1966: 3. On *Diary* 1.

Smith, Harrison. "Ladies in Turmoil." *Saturday Review* 30 Nov. 1946: 13.

Snitow, Ann. "Women's Private Writings: Anaïs Nin." *Notes from the Third Year*. New York: n.p., 1971. Rpt. in *Radical Feminism*. Ed. Anne Koedt, Ellen Levine, and Anita Rapone. New York: Quadrangle Books, 1973. 413-18.

Snyder, Robert. *Anaïs Nin Observed*. Chicago: Swallow Press, 1976.

Spacks, Patricia Meyer. "Free Women." *Hudson Review* 24.4 (Winter 1971-72): 559-73.

Spencer, Sharon. "Anaïs Nin." *Critical Survey of Short Fiction*. Englewood Cliffs, N.J.: Salem Press, 1981.

_____. "Anaïs Nin." *Critical Survey of Long Fiction*. Englewood Cliffs, N.J.: Salem Press, 1983.

_____. "Anaïs Nin: A Heroine for Our Time" *Journal of the Otto Rank Association* 12.1 (Summer 1977): 1-13.

_____. "Anaïs Nin's 'Continuous Novel': *Cities of the Interior*." Zaller 65-76.

_____. "The Art of Collage in Anaïs Nin's Writings." *Studies in the 20th Century* 16 (Fall 1975): 1-11.

_____. "*Cities of the Interior*: Femininity and Freedom." *Under the Sign of Pisces: Anaïs Nin and Her Circle*. 7.3 (Summer 1976): 9-16.

_____. *Collage of Dreams*. Chicago: Swallow, 1977. Expanded edition, New York: Harcourt Brace Jovanovich, 1981.

_____. "Delivering the Woman Artist from the Silence of the Womb: Otto Rank's Influence on Anaïs Nin." *The Psychoanalytic Review* 69.1 (Spring 1982): 111-29.

_____. "The Dream of Twinship in the Writings of Anaïs Nin." *Journal of the Otto Rank Association* 9.2 (Winter 1974-75): 81-90.

_____. "The Feminine Self: Anaïs Nin." *American Journal of Psychoanalysis* 50.1 (Mar. 1990): 57-62.

_____. " 'Femininity' and the Woman Writer: Doris Lessing's *The Golden Notebook* and the *Diary* of Anaïs Nin." *Women's Studies* 1 (1973): 247-57.

_____. Introduction. *Cities of the Interior*, by Anaïs Nin. Chicago: Swallow Press, 1974. x-xx.

_____. "The Music of the Womb: Anaïs Nin's 'Feminine' Writing." *Breaking the Sequence: Women's Experimental Fiction*. Ed. Ellen G. Friedman and Miriam Fuchs. Princeton, N.J.: Princeton University Press, 1989. 161-73.

_____. "A Novel Triangle: Anaïs Nin – Henry Miller – Otto Rank." *Journal of the Otto Rank Association* 14.2 (Winter 1979-80): 7-16

_____. *Space, Time, and Structure in the Modern Novel*. New York: New York University Press, 1971. Rpt. Chicago: Swallow Press, 1974.

_____, ed. *Anaïs, Art and Artists, a Collection of Essays*. Greenwood, Fl.: Penkevil, 1986.

Stern, Daniel. "The Diary of Anaïs Nin." *Studies in the Twentieth Century* 2 (Fall 1968): 39-43. The material here is almost identical with that in Stern's review, "Princess of the Underground," printed in *The Nation* 4 Mar. 1968: 311-13.

_____. "The Novel of Her Life: *The Diary of Anaïs Nin, Volume IV, 1944-1946*." *The Nation* 29 Nov. 1971: 570-72. Rpt. in Zaller 153-56.

Stimpson, Catharine R. "Authority and Absence: Women Write on Men." *Confrontation* 7 (Fall 1973): 81-91.

Stone, Albert E. "Becoming a Woman in Male America: Margaret Mead and Anaïs Nin." *Autobiographical Occasions and Original Acts: Versions of American Identity from Henry Adams to Nate Shaw*. Philadelphia: University of Pennsylvania Press, 1982. 190-230.

Stone, Jerome. "Fiction Note: The Psyche of the Huntress." *Saturday Review* 15 May 1954: 32. On *Spy*.

Struck, Karin. "Logbook of Liberation." Trans. Gunther Stuhlmann. *Anaïs: An International Journal* 6 (1988): 36-42.

"Stuff of Dreams." *Times Literary Supplement* 16 June 1961: 369. On *Seduction*.

Stuhlmann, Gunther. "Edward Titus Et Al." *Anaïs: An International Journal* 7 (1989): 113-18.

_____. "The Genesis of 'Alraune' – Some Notes on the Making of *House of Incest*." *Anaïs: An International Journal* 5 (1987): 115-23.

_____. "Into Another Language: Some Notes on Anaïs Nin's Work in Translation." *Anaïs: An International Journal* 1 (1983): 120-36.

_____. "Léon Pierre-Quint: Mastering the Art of Marcel Proust." *Anaïs: An International Journal* 6 (1988): 123-24.

_____. "What Did They Say? Writings about Anaïs Nin – An Informal Survey." *Anaïs: An International Journal* 1 (1983): 91-105.

_____. "Years of Friendship: Correspondence with Caresse Crosby, 1941-1970." *Anaïs: An International Journal* 2 (1984): 40-58.

Sugisaki, Kazuko. "The Dream and the Stage: A Study of the Dream in Anaïs Nin's Fiction and in Japanese Noh Drama." Spencer 87-99. Rpt. in *Anaïs: An International Journal* 6 (1988): 77-85.

Sukenick, Lynn. "Anaïs Nin: The Novel of Vision." Zaller 157-60.

_____. "The *Diaries* of Anaïs Nin." *Shenandoah* 17.3 (Spring 1976): 96-103.

Tibbetts, Robert A. "The Text of *On Writing*." *Under the Sign of Pisces: Anaïs Nin and Her Circle* 4.3 (Summer 1973): 1-7.

_____. "*A Spy in the House of Love*: A Note on the First Printings." *Under the Sign of Pisces: Anaïs Nin and Her Circle* 8.3 (Summer 1977): 1-4.

Trilling, Diana. "Fiction in Review." *The Nation* 26 Jan. 1946: 105-107. On *This Hunger*. Collected in her *Reviewing the Forties*. New York: Harcourt Brace Jovanovich, 1978. 143-47.

Tytell, John. "Anaïs Nin and 'The Fall of the House of Usher.' " *Under the Sign of Pisces: Anaïs Nin and Her Circle* 2.1 (Winter 1971): 5-11.

_____. *Passionate Lives: D. H. Lawrence, F. Scott Fitsgerald, Henry Miller, Dylan Thomas, Sylvia Plath – in Love*. Secaucus, N.J.: Carol Publications, 1991.

"*Under a Glass Bell and Other Stories*." *Virginia Kirkus Service* 15 Dec. 1947: 678.

Van der Elst, Marie-Claire. "The Birth of a Vocation." Spencer 5-11.

_____. "The Manuscripts of Anaïs Nin at Northwestern University." Hinz 59-63.

_____. "The Recognition of AN in France: A Selective Bibliography." *Under the Sign of Pisces: Anaïs Nin and Her Circle* 2.2 (Spring 1971): 10-12.

Vidal, Gore. "Taking a Grand Tour of Anaïs Nin's High Bohemia Via the Time Machine." *Los Angeles Times Book Review* 26 Sept. 1971: 1+. Rpt. as "The Fourth Diary of Anaïs Nin" in *Homage to Daniel Shays: Collected Essays 1952-1972*. New York: Random House, 1972. 403-9.

Waddington, Miriam. "Review of Anaïs Nin's *The Novel of the Future*." *Journal of the Otto Rank Association* 4.1 (June 1969): 54-60.

Wakoski, Diane. "The Craft of Plumbers, Carpenters & Mechanics: A Tribute to Anaïs Nin." *American Poetry Review* (Jan.-Feb.1973): 46-47. Rpt. as "A Tribute to Anaïs Nin" in Zaller 145-52.

Watson, Fred. "Allegories in 'Ragtime': Balance, Growth, Disintegration." *Under the Sign of Pisces: Anaïs Nin and Her Circle* 7.2 (Spring 1976): 1-5.

West, Paul. "D. H. Lawrence: Mystical Critic." *Southern Review* ns 1 (Jan. 1965): 210-28.

Wickes, George. *Americans in Paris, 1903-1939.* New York: Paris Review Editions/Doubleday, 1969.

Williams, William Carlos. " 'Men . . . Have No Tenderness': Anaïs Nin's 'Winter of Artifice.' " *New Directions No. 7.* Ed. James Laughlin. Norfolk, Conn.: New Directions, 1942. 429-36.

Wilson, Edmund. "Books – Doubts and Dreams: *Dangling Man* and *Under a Glass Bell.*" *New Yorker* 1 Apr. 1944: 78-82. Section on *Bell* rpt. in Zaller 3-4.

_____. "Books – Isherwood – Marquand – Anaïs Nin." *New Yorker* 10 Nov. 1945: 97-101. On *This Hunger.*

_____. "Books – A Note on Anaïs Nin." *New Yorker* 26 Nov. 1946: 114. On *Ladders.*

Wolcott, James. "Life Among the Ninnies." *New York Review of Books* 26 June 1980: 21. On *Diary* 7.

Wood, Lori A. "Between Creation and Destruction: Toward a New Concept of the Female Artist." *Anaïs: An International Journal* 8 (1990): 15-26.

Young, Marguerite. Rev. of *Anaïs Nin Reader. New York Woman* Sept. 1973: 12.

Young, Vernon. "Five Novels, Three Sexes, and Death." *Hudson Review* 1.3 (Fall 1948): 421-32. On *Bell*

Zaller, Robert. "Anaïs Nin and the Truth of Feeling." *Arts and Society* 10.2 (Summer 1973): 308-12. Rpt. in Zaller 177-83.

_____, ed. *A Casebook on Anaïs Nin.* New York: NAL/Meridian, 1974.

Zinnes, Harriet. "Anaïs Nin's Works Reissued." *Books Abroad* 37.3 (Summer 1963): 283-86. Rpt. as "The Fiction of Anaïs Nin" in Zaller 35-41.

_____. "Reading Anaïs Nin." *Carleton Miscellany* 14 (Fall-Winter 1973): 124-26. On *Reader.*

Index